Arlen Roth's

Complete Electric Guitar

by Arlen Roth

Doubleday & Company, Inc., Garden City, New York

Library of Congress Cataloging in Publication Data

Roth, Arlen.
    Arlen Roth's complete electric guitar.

    Discography: p. 142
    1. Guitar—Methods—Self-instruction.   2. Music,
Popular (Songs, etc.)—Instruction and study.   I. Title.
II. Title: Complete electric guitar.
MT588.R648   1984   83-8940
ISBN: 0-385-17620-1 (pbk.)

Arlen Roth's
Complete
Electric Guitar

*The author (left) on the summer of 1983 Simon and
Garfunkel tour. (Deborah Smith)*

This book is dedicated to the memory of Michael Bloomfield, whose playing had a profound influence on me during my formative years as an electric guitarist.

I would like to thank Joe Dalton, Hollis Cohen, John Peden, Jim Menick, Gerry Helferich, Doreen DeFlorio, Roy Wandelmaier, Arthur Schwartz, and all of my students for helping to make the creation of this book a rewarding process.

Very special love and thanks to my wife Deborah for all of her support, assistance, and love.

Contents

Introduction

Like many guitarists, I started playing on a cheap little something or other, with only two strings on it, that was lying around the house. My brother, ten years older than me and a real fifties teenager, bought it and, as is often the case, never pursued it much further. I'm grateful now for that errant purchase, along with the constant sounds of Elvis, Fats Domino, Frankie Lymon, and Buddy Holly that poured forth from his record player from 1956 to 1959 (when I was at the impressionable ages of four to seven). My father, an artist and great lover of flamenco guitar, saw that, despite my considerable progress on the violin, the guitar was the coming thing and, in my two-string improvisations, saw the spark he felt should one day ignite. Little did he or I know it would become my life.

After several months of classical guitar lessons when I was eleven, my family and I were on a trip to Cape Cod, where I saw an electric guitarist playing in a restaurant. He was easily seven years older than me, but I knew I was already better than he was; I was just dying to get my hands on that beauty he held so lovingly. With my parents there for moral support, I bravely walked up to him on his break and asked if I could play "just for a little while." Much to my surprise, he was immediately accommodating and, right from the first chord, I was hooked. This event, along with the love I already had for the Beatles (who had just reached our shores), set the stage for my long love affair with the electric guitar.

Much to the chagrin of my classical teacher, I bought a four-pickup Ideal guitar that was as flashy and garish as they came in 1964. Soon after that, I formed my first band, *Etc.,* early in 1965, and we made our debut at a talent show in our junior high school in the Bronx. All dressed in matching black velour, with our hair combed down over our eyes, we were immediately cut short by the two hundred girls who mobbed and chased us out into a pouring rainstorm, our guitars still in hand. We won the talent show, though we must have played for two minutes at the most. Needless to say, this experience told me something about the power potential of the electric guitar. A far cry from my Elvis imitations at the age of five with a tennis racquet in my hands!

I'm sure you do not need to be reminded of how powerful the electric guitar is. You must wish, however, to improve your ability and to extract *more* of this greatness. From the information contained in the pages that follow, I believe you'll be able to. I have found over the years that the way I learned to play the instrument is the best and most rewarding way for me to *teach* it. Rather than handing down one isolated lesson after another with no apparent goal in mind, each idea in this book represents a real step in the learning experience I have come to know. One major improvement is that this material is much more selective, in order to eliminate many of the trial-and-error processes I had to experience. You'll get plenty of chances to go through that on your own without my having to put you through any unnecessary maneuvers.

The electric guitar is surely a tool of expression, and its language is developed through what many consider unobtainable skills. Fear not—much of the necessary information is contained in this book. The fine art of string bending, for example, is a style I've made a study of for over fifteen years, yet hardly anywhere is this technique taught properly. We'll take an in-depth look into this and many other important means of expression.

I've included sections on rhythm, lead guitar, slide guitar, blues, fingerpicking, Nashville flat-picking and string-bending styles, rockabilly, early rock 'n' roll, R&B, heavy metal, rock, and many special "flash" techniques that have never been taught in books. There's also a section that discusses equipment, including pros and cons of various guitars, amplifiers, and accessories, plus a section on effects boxes and their applications.

Please remember that what *you* choose to do with this material is paramount. Aiding in the development of your own style of expression is the richest reward I can ever hope to achieve as your teacher. I also hope that having some of my experience rub off on you will help make this learning process even more enjoyable and rewarding.

I can recall one night, as I was coming off the stage after a rousing, sweaty radio broadcast concert, a young kid yelled out to me on my way back to the dressing room, "Hey, Arlen! I'm really good and I want to do what you're doing. What should I do?" Gathering my thoughts, I replied, "Get out there and *do it*. Play, play, play. I can tell you that one good thing will always lead to another if you truly love your instrument."

I truly hope you enjoy this book.

ARLEN ROTH
New York City

1

Reading Tablature and Symbols

For those who cannot read music and as an additional aid to those who can, I've provided guitar tablature below all of the standard notation in this book. The six horizontal lines represent the six strings of the guitar, with low E at the bottom:

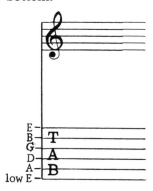

A number intersected by the line represents the fret at which the left hand depresses the string. For example, here is how an open C chord would be represented:

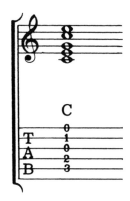

SYMBOLS

An arched line with an **s** over it tying two notes together means that there is a *slide* between the two notes. This will be used in the book to represent sliding with the finger.[1] The slide symbol also means that only the first note is plucked, while the second is created by the slide itself:

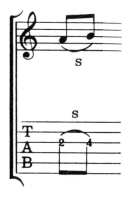

If the arch has an **h** over it, this illustrates a *hammer-on*. Here, the right hand picks only the first note. The second is sounded by "hammering" with a finger of the left hand higher up on the fingerboard:

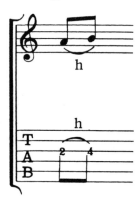

The same arch with a **p** over it represents a *pull-off*, or *left-hand pluck*. In this case, the second note, which is higher up on the string,

[1] For an in-depth look at using bottleneck techniques to play slide guitar, consult *Slide Guitar*, by Arlen Roth.

1

is plucked by the same finger that holds down the **first note:**

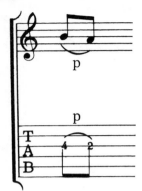

An arched line with a **B** over it represents a *bend.* A bend enables you to raise the pitch of the note by pushing or pulling the string toward or away from you at the same fret. Here, two notes are tied together, playing the first note, then bending that note to create the note that is in parentheses. Note that the bent note has a **time value, just as the** unbent note does:

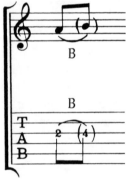

An **R** signals a release of a bend. This usually occurs right after a bend, reversing the original action:

At times the release may occur alone. Here, the string is bent *before* picking the release note:

A straight line pointing up or down *toward* a note means you slide *to* that note from an optional point below or above it. A straight line pointing up or down *away* from a note means you should slide *from* that note without **sounding another specific note with the slide:**

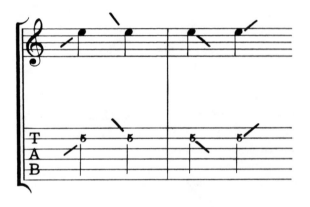

A note played with *vibrato* will have a wavy line above it. The proper technique of vibrato **will be discussed later on in the book:**

Fundamentals of Electric Guitar Playing

HOLDING THE INSTRUMENT

STANDING This is the most common position for playing the electric guitar, especially in performing situations. From time to time, the studio musician will also find that a certain song or a particular solo might require standing up for him to physically get more "into it." I can recall many a take saved by assuming the standing position and putting the right energy into my part, which helped to ignite the rest of the band to do the same.

The actual position is as individual as the player. (I can mimic many guitarists, just the way I could imitate the various baseball stars in the batter's box when I was a kid.) The most common position is with the weight on the back foot and with the neck of the guitar raised high enough to relieve the fretting hand of any weight burden. Occasionally you will find the desire to rock your weight back and forth from foot to foot. This is important to avoid strain on your back. It's also important to avoid the hunched-over position that can be brought on by long periods of standing with a heavy guitar such as the popular Les Paul model.

SITTING When practicing or recording in the studio, this is the most commonly used position. It's important, again, not to be too hunched over from your neck or upper back, to alleviate any fatigue that may be setting

in. It's far better to let the lower back muscles assume the work and let you achieve the slight, natural angle needed in playing while seated.

THE PICK

There are a wide variety of sizes, shapes, and thicknesses available. Various types are favored by various players. The really small teardrop-shaped picks are preferred by the single-note jazz-style players, who require rapid playing, while the large triangular picks are used by the "heavy metal" power-chord players.

The pick I would most recommend for overall adaptability is the common semitriangular pick with two rounded corners and of medium thickness.

This photo illustrates the proper holding position, between thumb and forefinger, letting just enough of the pick show so you can

maintain good control over it without having to grip it too tightly.

SETTING THE GUITAR UP FOR BEST RESULTS

Making the guitar play and feel right for you (or "setting it up," as it's often called) is something every guitarist should at least know enough about so as to avoid making useless trips to the repair shop. Not to mention that great byproduct of know-how: saving money! There are two crucial elements that make up this setup of your guitar. They are the "action" of the instrument, or the feeling that results from the distance between string and fret; and the intonation, or accuracy of pitch on the fingerboard. These two elements, action and intonation, are controlled by five factors: the strings, the frets, the nut, the bridge height, and the bridge position.

Many people when encountering an electric guitar for the first time, especially a solidbody, invariably notice how much easier it is to play than their acoustic instrument. This is usually due to the ease of action and relative lightness of string gauge when compared to the more cumbersome acoustic-guitar strings. The one thing they quickly learn, however, is that because of amplification, the electric guitar is an instrument of powerful expression that requires a great deal of control. In terms of the action, I'm of the firm belief that the strings should not be too close to the fingerboard if you expect to get the full range of capabilities out of your instrument. The higher the strings, the less fret buzz you'll experience and the more string you'll have to grab onto for bending and vibrato. The actual height of your action is such a personal matter that I wouldn't even begin to suggest any specific height, only that you should be careful not to set it too high or too low. The string height is usually set at the bridge (providing it's adjustable); however, the nut can sometimes play a part in this if it's cut too deep or not deep enough. If it is set too deeply, the only true recourse is to have a repairman replace it. Bone is the most preferable material, though I highly recommend brass for bridges because of its superior sustaining properties.

Factory-installed frets of a new assembly-line-type guitar are rarely in truly "playable" condition, particularly along the edges of the fingerboard, where there may still be some sharp edges due to the fret wire being clipped and not smoothed out properly.

In used or vintage instruments, the most common fret problems arise simply from plain old use. You'll often find old guitars with grooves in the frets, especially from the frequently played open chord positions; many times the frets will be almost worn down to the fingerboard. If either of these is the case, a new fret job by a real pro that includes grinding and polishing the frets, or "dressing" them, as many luthiers (lute makers) call it, will give the fingerboard new life.

There is one important rule to follow when thinking about string gauges; the heavier the string, the richer the sound.

I can recall hearing this advice in a guitar shop I loved to hang out in when I was a teenager. I used to play every vintage beauty that came in there, and was already well on my way to becoming the "string-bending fool" I am today. I just loved to string my '52 Les Paul up with a set of slinky .009's and go nuts with it. I was, however, getting to be so adept at bending the strings subtly that the guy in the store felt I could handle the heavier, standard "light" set that had a high E string of .010 gauge. He was right, and I was immediately amazed with the richer tones I was producing. Even to this day, I have students boasting ten years of experience, still flailing away on some "rubber bands" and not getting nearly the sound out of their instrument they could. So I tell them as I tell you: try to use, at the lightest, a set of strings with these gauges: high E, .010; B, .013; G, .017; D, .026; A, .036; low E, .046.

SETTING THE INTONATION

Providing your neck is straight and no problems exist such as warpage, you should properly set the intonation of your guitar. What you will actually be doing is lengthening or shortening the distance of the string between the bridge and the nut. On all adjustable bridges this is done with either a screwdriver or an Allen wrench, depending on the particular guitar. What you want to do is make the note at the twelfth fret of each string exactly match the harmonic at that very same fret. (The harmonic is a high, bell-like tone produced by plucking the string and, as it vibrates, touching it gently at, in this case, the twelfth fret.) This does require something of an "ear," and many people, most notably luthiers, utilize visual aids such as strobe tuners to be absolutely accurate. If the fretted note is flat to the harmonic, shortening the string length would do the trick. If the same fretted note is sharp to the harmonic, turning the adjusting screw in the opposite, lengthening direction would set matters straight.

2
Rhythm Guitar Techniques

When I was eighteen and starting to do sessions, I had already put a few years of serious lead guitar playing under my belt. The more sessions I played, however, particularly record dates, the more apparent it became to me that the disciplines of rhythm guitar were essential to my success in the recording field. More often than not, these recording situations require the guitarist to lay down a rhythm part along with the rest of the rhythm section. This is usually done "live," and mistakes can be corrected only if your amplifier is isolated enough so as to avoid "leakage" into the other microphones. Obviously in these situations the guitarist can find himself at fault for ruining a take if the other section players have done their jobs well; the tape must roll again because of his mistake.

Remember that rhythm guitar is not to be taken lightly. Even the lead guitarist must usually play only a partial-chord rhythm part behind the vocal or other lead instrument. Needless to say, rhythm guitar is *the* foundation for all lead playing, and you cannot consider yourself a well-rounded guitarist without these rhythm guitar disciplines.

In the section that follows, we'll cover the many facets of rhythm guitar, and because it is so effective when discussing an art form, we'll use the chronological approach to the history of the electric rhythm guitar to better illustrate how it has evolved. Now let's start playing.

The Movable Chord Positions

One of the most important techniques for the rhythm guitarist to be aware of is smooth movement of one chord position to another. When you study the basic open chord positions, and later move on to the more difficult, closed positions (explained below), you'll see that the open positions are repeated all over the neck. These movable positions, namely E, A, C7, C9, and G, will be discussed in this chapter.

E-FORM BARRE CHORDS

The first closed position one usually encounters in the course of learning the guitar is also for many the most difficult: the ever-important E-form barre chord. The first movement of this position up the neck results in an F chord, because we are now one half step up from open E. In the photo of this position, note the slight curving of my index, or "barring," finger. This is enabling the boney

side of my finger to touch the strings, producing a clearer, stronger tone. If you're experiencing a dull sound, particularly on the high E and B strings, chances are you're not pressing hard enough (understandable; it will hurt for a while) or you're using the fleshier,

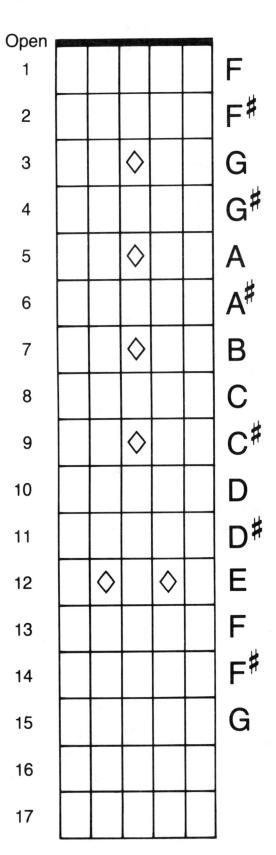

Diagram 1

"palm" of your finger, to create a duller tone. Now, according to the chart (Diagram 1), you'll see how moving this barre position up the neck will produce the full range of major chords. First fret, F; second fret, F#, etc. Note that at the twelfth fret of the guitar, we have now reached a new octave and are back at E again. Therefore, the thirteenth fret would be the next-higher octave of the F chord we previously played at the first fret.

A-FORM BARRE CHORDS

Just as there are an open E and an open A, there are an E barre and an A barre. The A form is less frequently seen, particularly in its complete form, but it's just as important. One of the major differences between this barre chord and the E form is that the index finger should now cover only five strings, from the A to the high E string. Also keep in mind that the barring finger need not work as hard as it did in the case of the E form: Only the A string and the high E string are being sounded by the barre; the B, the G, and the D are being **fretted by the other three fingers.**

Diagram 2 shows the names of the chords as the A-form barre is moved up the neck. Keep in mind that certain open strings may be added to the partial barre chord when the opportunity arises. For example, when you've

Open					
1					A#
2					B
3			◇		C
4					C#
5			◇		D
6					D#
7			◇		E
8					F
9			◇		F#
10					G
11					G#
12		◇		◇	A
13					A#
14					B
15					C
16					
17					

Diagram 2

reached the E chord, at the seventh fret, you can play it with the open low-E string, thereby giving the chord a more powerful, "split octave" sound.

These chord exercises illustrate the use of combined chord forms. In the first we see the combination of open E, open A, and closed B.

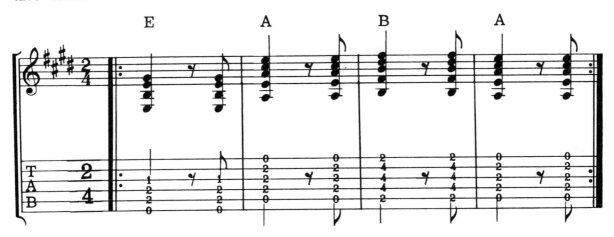

Here we see how the same type of progression in a new key can be achieved by an all-barre chord situation. Remember to cover only five strings for the A forms. Your barring finger should also be doing some silent work by lightly touching the low E string and damping it out so it will not clash with the other notes. This technique of damping is a crucial aspect of guitar playing, and you'll see its increasing importance as we progress through this book.

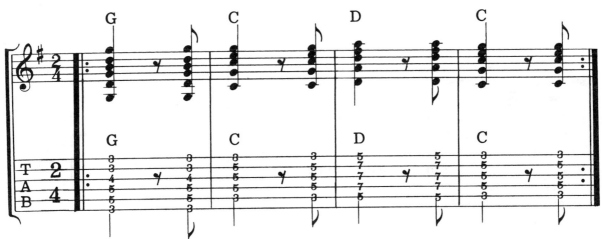

SEVENTH-CHORD BARRES

Just as the open positions of E and A have their seventh inversions, so do their barre-chord counterparts. Here is the G7 barre chord with the pinkie taken off the D string to expose the barred F note on the third fret.

You also have the option of using your pinkie to add the higher octave of the seventh to the chord, as in this picture. Remember that this seventh can always be found on the B **string three frets above the barre.**

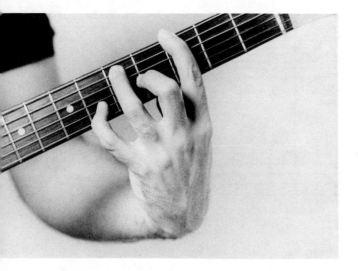

THE C7 MOVABLE CHORD POSITION

The C7 position is particularly intriguing because it utilizes only the four middle strings—a position usually reserved for chords that include open strings. Damping is crucial to the proper movement of this chord form, and it must occur in two places as a natural by-product of the chord position itself. For instance, the high E string is cut out by the index finger, which must cross over the E string to play the B string. The second damping occurs when the low E string is stopped by either the ring finger, which is playing the A string next to it, or the tip of the thumb, which is just curling over the edge of the fingerboard. Try them and see which damping technique feels **the more natural to you.**

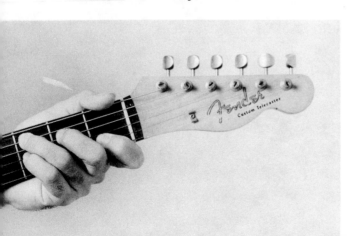

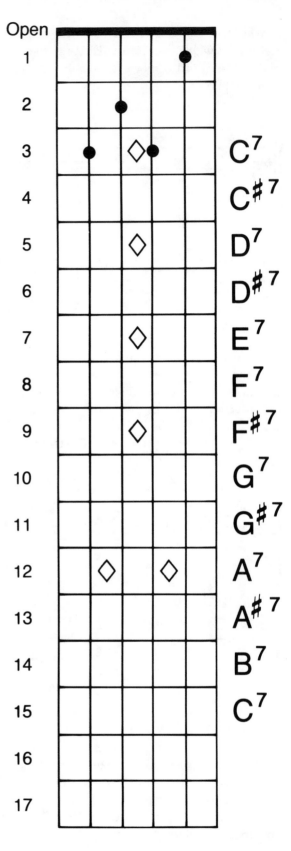

Diagram 3

Try moving this closed chord position up the neck cleanly, as indicated in Diagram 3.

The following exercise illustrates the use of two further simplified forms of barres we've been playing in combination with the new closed C7 form you've just learned. The first two are E and A forms that use the top four strings only. Note how these particular chord forms move into each other with great fluidity.

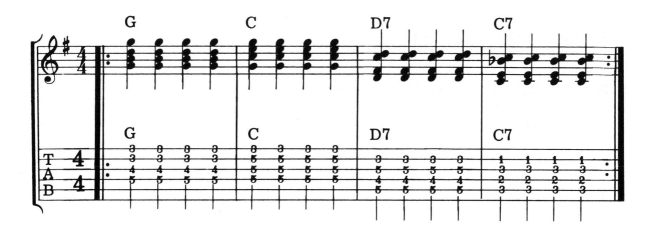

Early Blues and Rock 'n' Roll Styles

Recalling the blues and rock electric guitar styles that flourished in the fifties, it was the guitar that was for the first time truly coming into the spotlight of a music so vibrant that it took an electric instrument to make its message loud and clear. Performers like Chuck Berry, Buddy Holly, Bo Diddley, Carl Perkins, Cliff Gallup, and Scotty Moore were playing an exciting blend of lead and rhythm with new dimensions that were to permanently change the face of music history.

Early blues music, one of the major roots of rock 'n' roll, was almost always played in a twelve-bar format. This is of course the famous "twelve-bar blues" we always hear of and is an essential element in any guitarist's vocabulary. Since blues is of the question/question/answer format both lyrically and instrumentally, the use of this twelve-bar format over and over again becomes apparent the more one plays blues music.

The following diagram illustrates the twelve-bar blues as it would appear for the key of E. The last two bars are called the "turnaround," a part of the progression that actually serves to turn the piece around and bring it back to the beginning.

Another term used to describe this type of blues is the "I, IV, V" progression. You will notice that in the chord sequence we just illustrated, there were primarily three chords used: E, A, and B. These chords are the I, IV, and V of the key of E. Simply defined, the I chord is always the key you are in, or the *tonic*. The IV chord in this case is the fourth note away in the major scale (whole step, whole step, half . . .) of the key you are playing in; hence E, F#, G#, A (fourth note). This fourth chord is also called the *subdominant*. The V is called the *dominant* chord.

The following useful chart lists the various keys and their subdominant and dominant chords.

| I | IV | V |
root (tonic)	sub-dominant	dominant
A	D	E
B♭(A#)	E♭(D#)	F
B	E	F#(G♭)
C	F	G
D♭(C#)	G♭(F#)	A♭(G#)
D	G	A
E♭(D#)	A♭(G#)	B♭(A#)
E	A	B
F	B♭(A#)	C
F#(G♭)	B	C#(D♭)
G	C	D
A♭(G#)	D♭(C#)	E♭(D#)

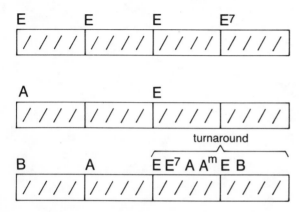

Diagram 4

Diagram 5

THE "SHUFFLES"

One of the most popular methods of conveying a twelve-bar blues is through the "shuffle" style. This is a classic rhythm part heard very often in the playing of people like Chuck Berry, Jimmy Reed, and Elmore James. It's still being heavily used today and is often one of the first enjoyable learning experiences for **any contemporary rock guitarist.**

Shuffle licks usually consist of the two bottommost bass notes of a given chord, providing these two notes are a root note and its fifth; e.g., E and B.

Here is your first shuffle exercise, in the key of A. I've chosen this key because the I, IV, and V chords (A, D, and E) can all be played in the open position. Remember to alternate the shuffle notes (second to fourth frets) between your first and third fingers, and to use all *down* strokes with your picking hand.

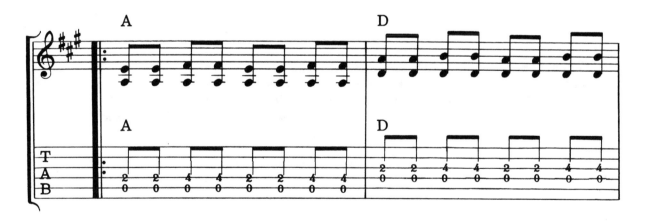

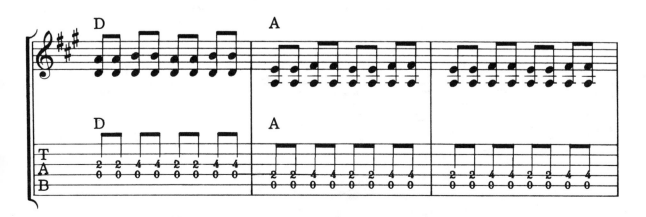

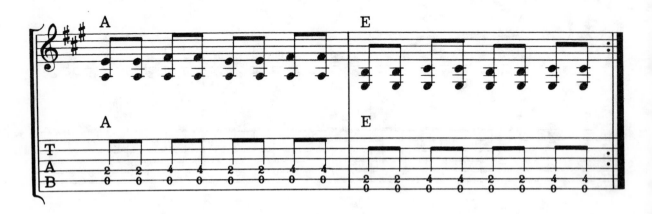

This next exercise illustrates a progression involving three chords (G, C, and D) that are being played in their closed and partial barre positions. That is to say that they utilize no open strings, and consist of less than six notes. In this piece we see that the G chord is based on the E-form barre, while the C and D are based on the A-form barre position.

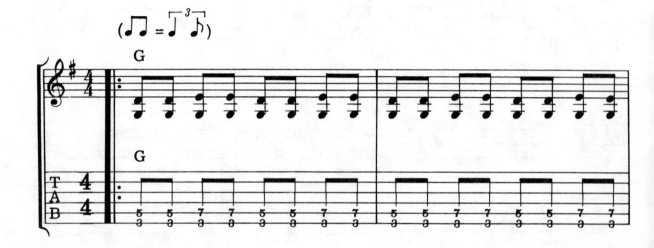

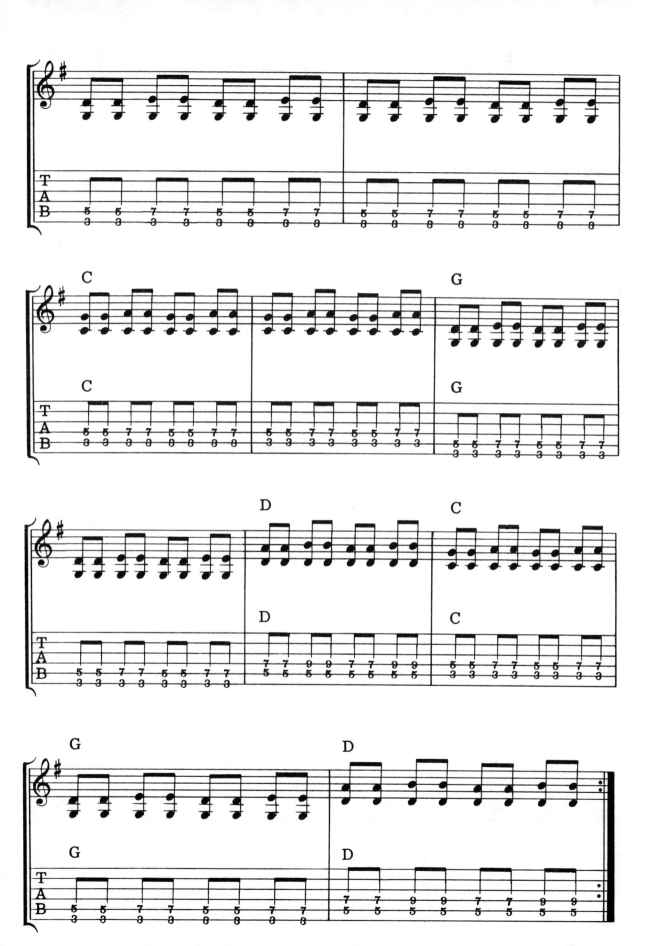

This final twelve-bar-blues shuffle exercise illustrates the additional use of a seventh note sometimes added to the shuffle to further accentuate the changing of a chord and also a "turnaround" lick at the end of the progression. Take note that this progression in E combines both open and closed shuffle positions.

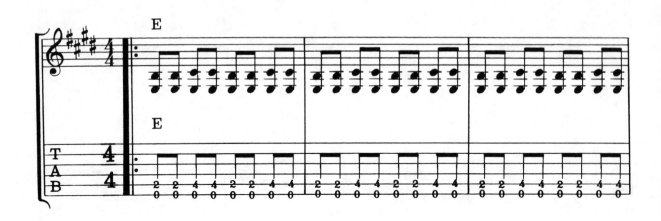

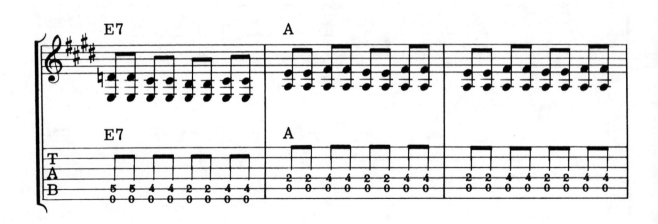

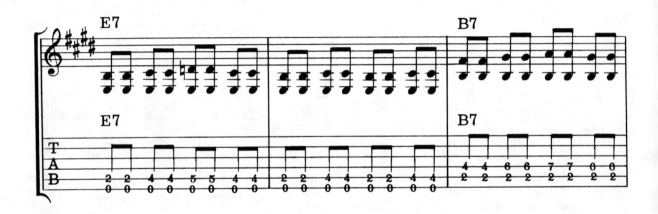

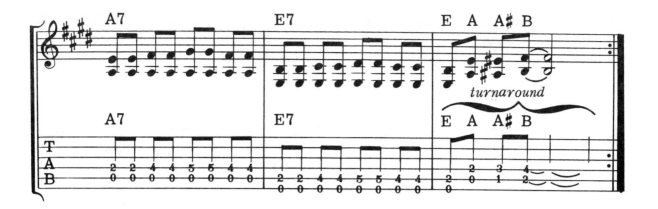

THE HARMONY SHUFFLE

These exercises illustrate exactly what the heading says: shuffle licks played in harmony. Each open chord position now has a note that moves in perfect harmony with the original moving shuffle note. Because of their unique properties, and the fact that several of them introduce new techniques to this book, all four harmony shuffle positions will be covered one at a time before we actually play a full-length exercise.

THE E POSITION

In this position, you'll notice that the G string will be the *moving harmony* line to the A string, and that the D string is now left open, creating an E7 chord. This note (D) is best "damped" out however, and this can be created by the index finger lightly touching the D string while it moves along the G string. Therefore, in this lick as you can see, the index finger never leaves the G string, while the second and third fingers alternate on the A string. Again, all down strokes would best suit this particular pattern.

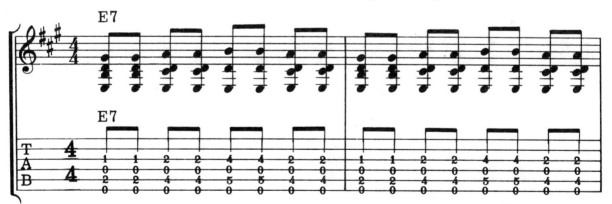

THE A POSITION

This position is special because it introduces the idea of using a partial barre to create an open A chord. In this case, the index finger lies across the D, G, and B strings, while pressing on the high E string just hard enough to damp it out of the chord. The second position of this harmony lick is really a partial form of D put on top of our original second-fret barre, leaving the barred note on the G string (A) to continue ringing and to become part of the new D chord. The barre is finally abandoned for the third position, which is best played by the second and third fingers.

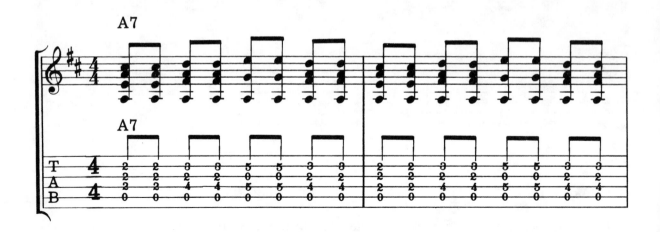

THE D POSITION

This position introduces a new way of playing an open D chord where the second frets on both the G and high E strings are covered by a first-finger barre, leaving just the third fret on the B string to be played by the second finger. The second position, actually a G chord over a D bass, uses the first finger as a barre on the *top* two strings instead, with the second finger crossing over to the G string. Keep practicing this particular move until it becomes fluid.

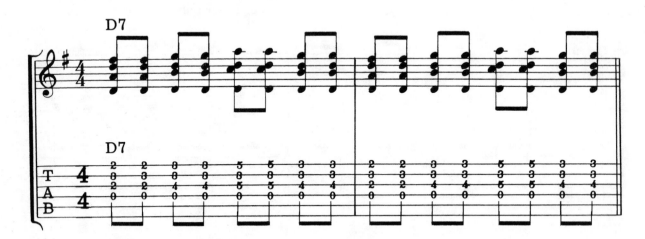

THE G POSITION

The open G position is really the same as the open A, only moved down two frets, thereby eliminating the necessity for any barring but losing the convenience of an open bass note such as A. The second position, you will see, is really a C chord over a G bass, while in the third position your index finger must come all the way around to play the same G bass that was previously being played by the third finger.

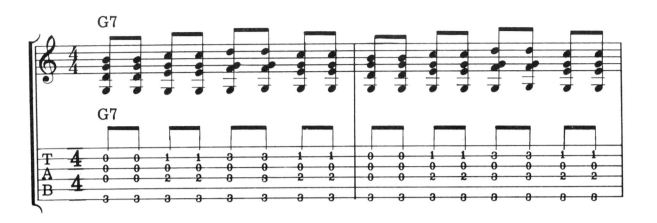

Here is a twelve bar harmony shuffle exercise for the key of A, whose I, IV, and V chords are A, D, and E. In the case of each chord, this piece utilizes an alternation between the bass notes and the chords.

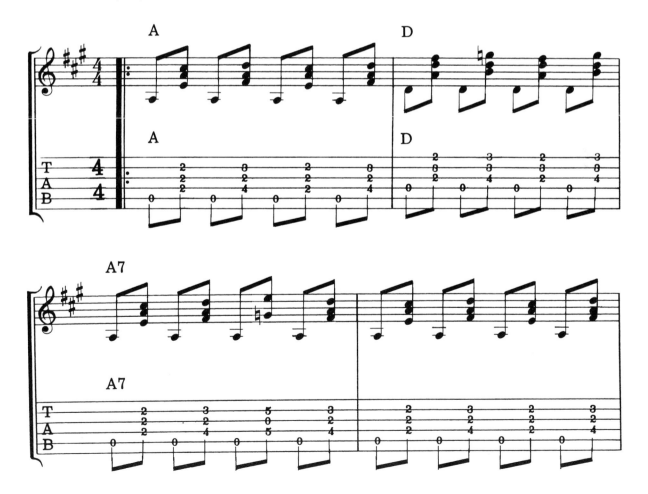

THE "BO DIDDLEY" LICK

Bo Diddley made his mark on the blues and rock 'n' roll world by developing a unique, hard-driving, and many times flashy style of rhythm playing that was at the pulse of all his songs. His true signature lick was a rhythmic strum that resembles the old "shave and a haircut, two bits." Songs like "Bo Diddley," "Mona," and Buddy Holly's "Not Fade Away"

exemplify this approach to the classic rhythm-guitar lick. As hard-driving as this riff is, it's really an exercise in right- and left-hand control. What physically happens in a lick like this is the left hand only depresses the chord when needed, while the right hand keeps up a constant and strong rhythm. Therefore you should *press* the chords down only when needed, while during silent passages you lift the chord position up just enough to help in the damping of those very same strings.

HEEL DAMPING

One technique that sometimes has been used as a purely "flash" technique, yet is an indispensable part of any guitarist's repertoire, is the art of "heel damping." This is the sound heard so often when a guitarist wishes to cut the sustaining of the string off, creating a more abrasive and staccato effect. Many times this has been traditionally used in country guitar circles. In fact, Merle Travis, the legendary fingerpicker, will use this technique to damp the bass notes of a song while the lead or melody notes are allowed to ring true. This creates an even greater degree of separation between the two sounds.

The photo that follows illustrates the proper position for heel damping. Please remember that it's important to be subtle with this technique, by not pressing down too hard on the strings or creating the damp too far from where the strings actually meet the bridge.

Both of these errors would tend to make the affected notes become too sharp in pitch, and possibly even too dulled. The "Bo Diddley" lick we just practiced would be good to try with the "heel damp," as would the shuffle-rhythm licks we've covered.

Keep on practicing these rhythm techniques till you feel as comfortable as possible with them.

RHYTHM-AND-BLUES TECHNIQUES

More than any other aspect of guitar playing, the one quality required by all in rhythm-and-blues music is *discipline*. Of course this applies to all forms of music, but rhythm and blues usually shoves the guitarist to the back seat of the bus. This is not to say guitar is unimportant, just that it is a part of the *rhythm section*—the *pulse* of the music. Any guitarist who's listened to the music of James Brown, or the later disco craze, can't help but be amazed by the repetitious parts required of the guitar.

Early in my career, I was called on for far more rhythm-and-blues dates than I cared to do. I never shunned the work, but I often found myself faced with an irate and impatient producer who couldn't stand my lack of interest in this style of playing. Being young and *hot*, my first tendency was to overplay, and because of my desire for originality, I developed a block about playing a consistent, sometimes monotonous rhythm part. Don't worry if you suffer from these symptoms. This tendency to play more than is required in your developing years is a healthy one, especially if you want to keep getting called to the studios!

Actually, all the techniques we've covered so far are, historically, R&B styles. (Chuck Berry and Bo Diddley are rhythm-and-blues artists.) I'm using the term to define the more intricate and sophisticated sound that took hold of black music from about Sam Cooke's debut on to the present. As R&B has evolved over the years, including the sounds of Otis Redding, Wilson Pickett, Motown, James Brown, Aretha Franklin, it's gone through many phases. As it entered the seventies and eighties (a guitar-dominated period), the guitar began taking a more and more important role, influencing the overall scope of the instrument in the process. It is this evolution that will help guide the lessons that follow in this chapter.

THE EARLY ARPEGGIOS

One of the most soulful applications of rhythm guitar in the early music of such performers as Sam Cooke and Otis Redding was the gospel-rooted *arpeggiated* parts, played by people like Steve Cropper and Bobby Womack. These arpeggios are really no more than chords played one note at a time. The staccato effect is important in this style, and for this reason it's usually played in a barred form, many times with heel damping employed. Songs like "Unchained Melody," "Bring It on Home to Me," "I've Been Loving You," and even the mid-sixties Animals version of "House of the Rising Sun" are reminders of memorable guitar parts that were *arpeggios*. Here, just to get going, is an exercise in arpeggios that is the I, VI, IV, V progression so prevalent in the songs of the fifties and early sixties that followed the earlier I, IV, V progressions of the blues and blues-influenced artists. Play it all with down strokes, yet with a light enough touch so as not to be overbearing on the notes. This heavy-handedness can be a problem when notes are this close to one another, so try your best to be careful.

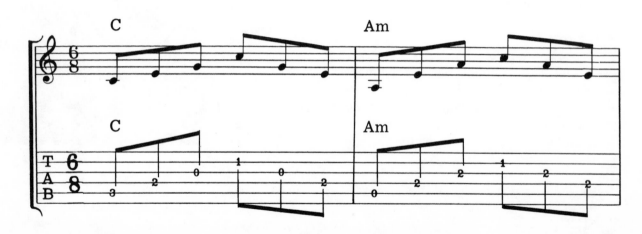

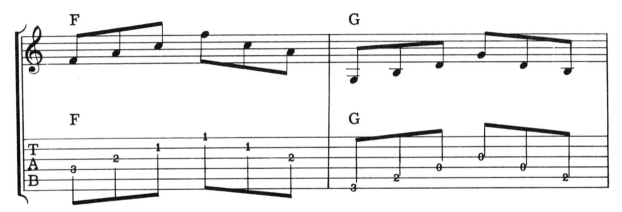

Steve Cropper, the guitarist in the legendary rhythm section of the Stax-Volt record days in Memphis, who played on the records of Booker T. and the MGs, Otis Redding, Wilson Pickett, and other greats, is one of the premier exponents of this and other soulful R&B techniques. His use of the arpeggio in soulful, slow ballads is one of his most recognizable and most imitated trademarks. In some of Otis Redding's most memorable tunes, like "Try a Little Tenderness," "I've Got Dreams to Remember," and "I've Been Loving You," this great backup technique can be heard at its best.

Before we go on to the exercise which is in a classic early R&B progression, please take note of the use of "slides" at the beginning of several chords that help accent the drama of this particular style. Also try it with a slightly "heel-damped" effect, a classic approach to this style as well. Since this passage should be played relatively slowly, alternated picking would be advisable. This type of playing has influenced many of the younger players, and it can be heard quite often in the playing of Keith Richards of the Rolling Stones.

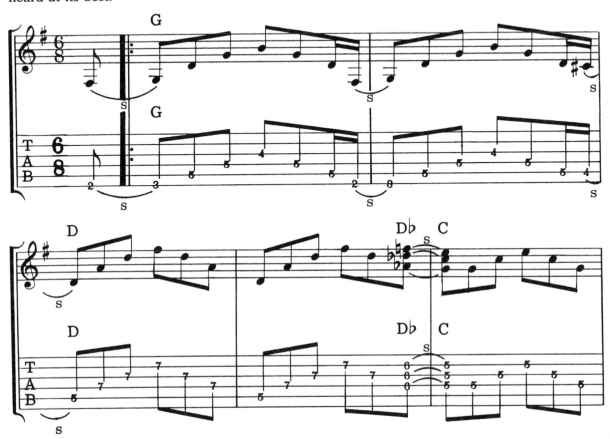

"THE HOUSE OF THE RISING SUN"

This song, a classic southern tune, was spotlighted by a group called the Animals during the early-sixties British music invasion. It had a recognizable arpeggiated guitar part that had everybody's junior high school rock band (mine included) anxiously learning it. Here's the fabled part in the key of A minor.

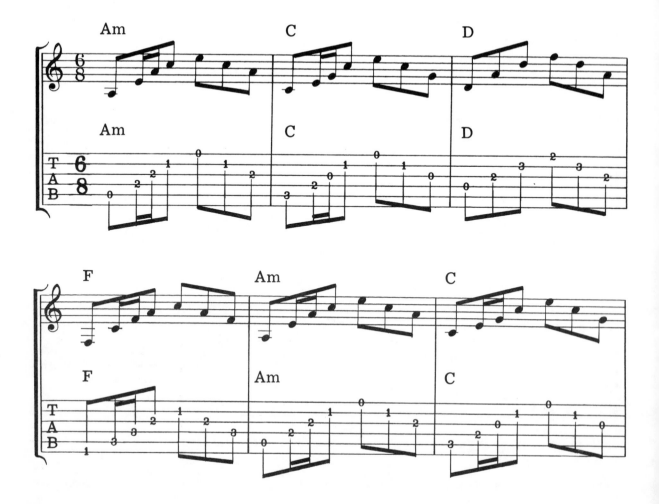

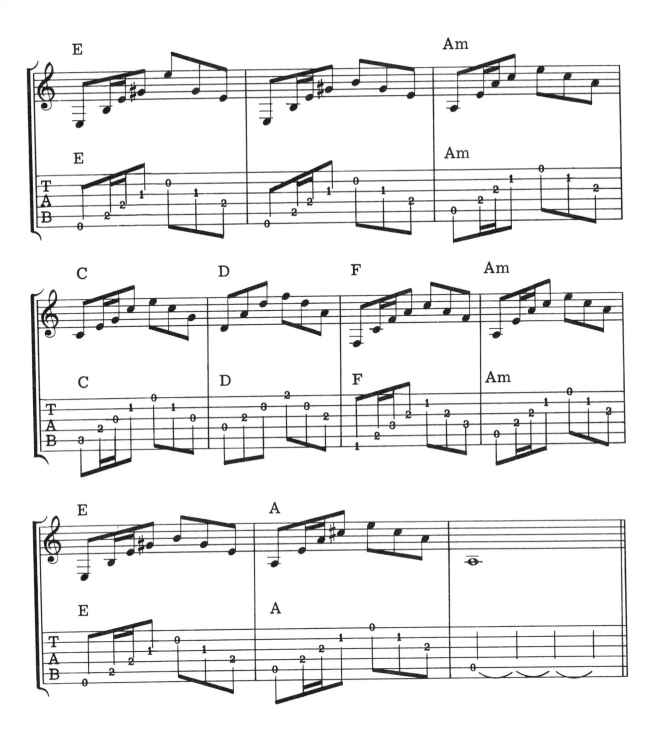

FUNKY RHYTHMS

When I think of "funk" or "funky music," the first thing that comes to mind is that the arrangements are usually more complex-sounding than you would expect from the number of instruments that are playing them. This is because each player's part commonly comprises a few elements that seem to go around in some predetermined cycle. Keep in mind, however, that these parts are often composed on the spot by the musicians. This composing creates a part that sounds more like a combination of lead and rhythm guitar styles (though the player is rarely a "hot" lead player in his own right). Cornell Dupree, a great New York R&B player, has been a leading exponent of this style for many years, not to mention Steve Cropper, and Eric Gale. Jimi Hendrix also had strong schooling in this department, and it was quite evident even through the psychedelic haze of his playing that his roots were thoroughly Rhythm and Blues.

One of the most evident characteristics of funky R&B playing is that one rarely hears single-note work. If there is any, it usually precedes a rhythm chord lick, acting in essence as a bass run. One classic example of this style is what I call the "Funky Broadway" lick. This is based on the playing of Steve Cropper on Wilson Pickett's hit record of the same name. These runs illustrate this combined bass-note and rhythm-lick style I've been talking about, and are played here in open E position and in the closed C7 position of E as well.

Here's the first "Funky Broadway" lick in open E. Please try to use all down strokes for the bass runs, while doing a quick down-up-down pattern for the rhythmic "answer."

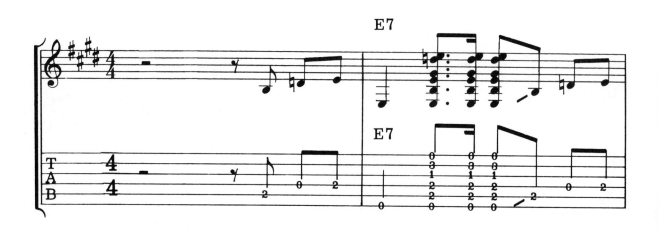

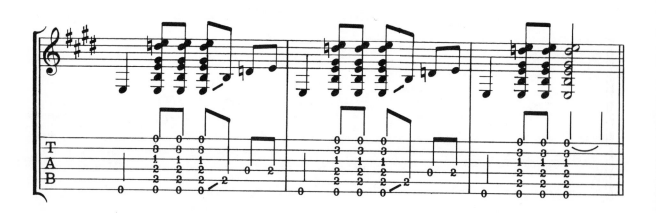

26

The next pattern, though more difficult and in a "closed" position, is really the more commonly used of the two. Use the same picking patterns as indicated before, and note how this chord, being a "closed" position of E7, enables the open low E string to come into play, thereby giving the chord a wider "spread" in terms of octaves than most chord forms can achieve.

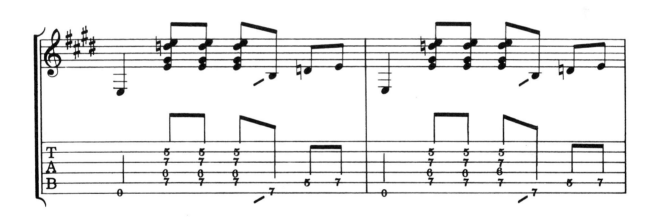

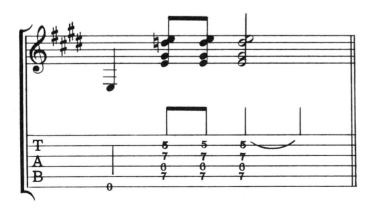

The use of a "hammer-on," where the note is created by your fretting finger as opposed to your pick, is also useful in funky playing.

One very commonly used is the G# hammer-on as part of an open E chord:

Note here that to achieve the same hammer-on in the closed position we must use the first finger to cover the note that is played just before the hammer-on:

SLIDING THE CHORDS

These same "closed" chord positions are very often slid either partially or completely to help accent the beginning of a new bar, or anticipate or syncopate the rhythm. This exercise provides a good picture of some of the things that can be done.

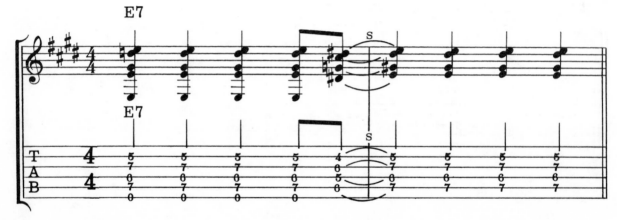

Shuffles are often heard in funky R&B, and sliding the two note positions these licks start on at the right times can really help to beef up a rhythm part.

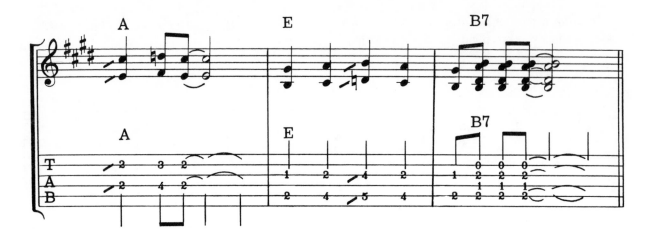

THE C9 CHORD POSITION IN BLUES AND R&B

First, this space offers me a great opportunity to repeat my advice to each of my new students: If you are playing the C9 chord position with your first, second, and third fingers, you are doing it *all wrong!*

Rather, try the second, third, and fourth fingers. One simple illustration will show you how natural this position is: First, play an open C chord, now add your pinkie to the third fret on the G string, making it a C7. Now, to make it a C9, all you need to do is lay that same pinkie down across all three top strings, starting at the B*b* note your pinkie was just playing. There you have it: It's also much easier to now take this position and go back to your open G position, another chord so often misplayed by using the wrong finger configuration (the second finger on the low E string). The better position is with the third finger playing the low G note and the pinkie playing the high G.

THE C9 CHORD POSITION IN CHICAGO BLUES

When I first started listening to blues artists like T-Bone Walker, Buddy Guy, and Otis Rush, I noticed that while their guitar playing contained very little in the way of chord work, their rhythm parts more often than not contained certain three-note slides that, at the time, I could define only as being "smooth." I knew these had to be rooted in some true chord form, and finally one day I discovered the C9 chord position and the whole picture made much more sense to me.

Seeing that this particular lick can exist both in partial and in full chord forms, I thought I'd illustrate them to you in just the order I learned them. Here, first, is the partial form, containing the slides that are heard so often in the rhythm parts of the Chicago blues players who use these positions:

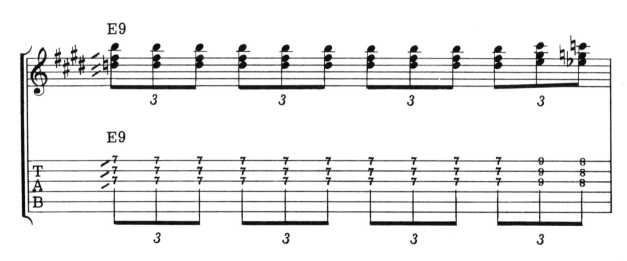

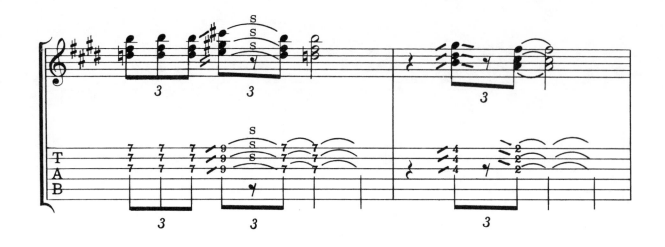

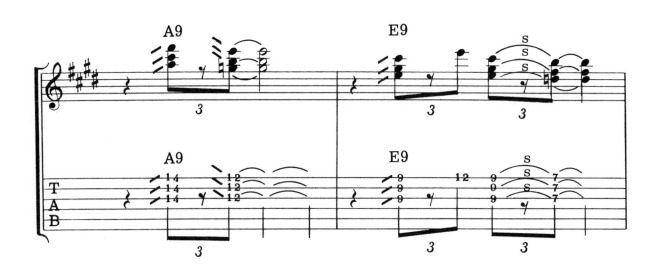

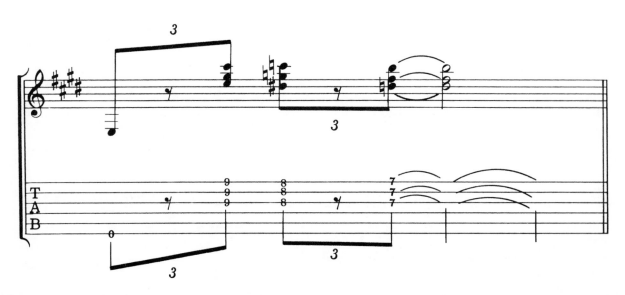

Here is the same progression using the full chord form. I've placed the slides in the same places; you should experiment to see if it feels better to use your pinkie or to jump across with your index finger to play them.

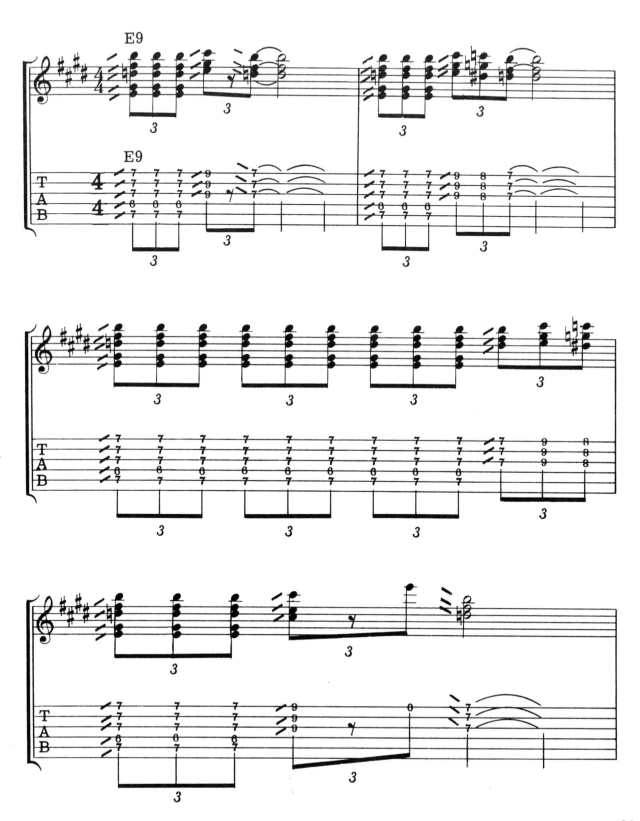

33

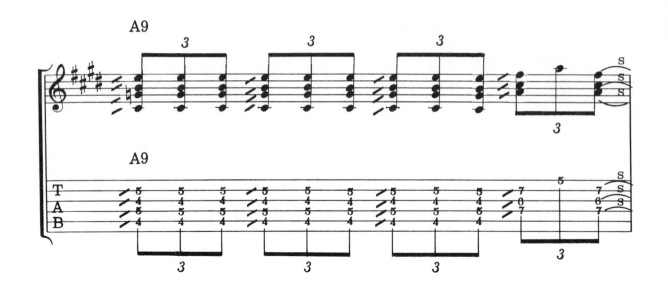

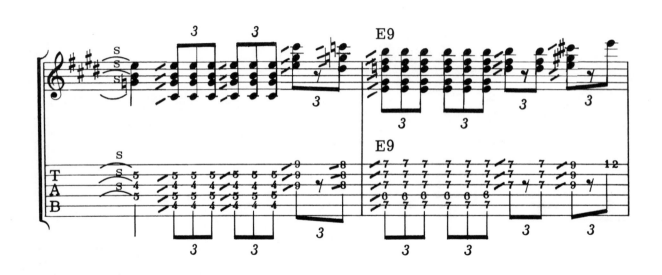

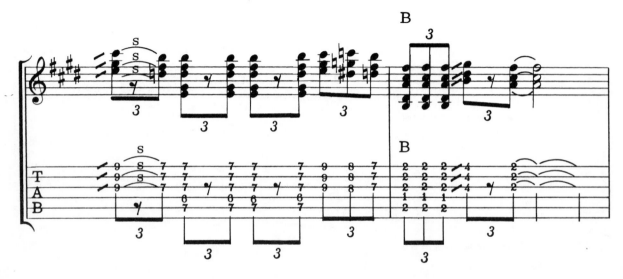

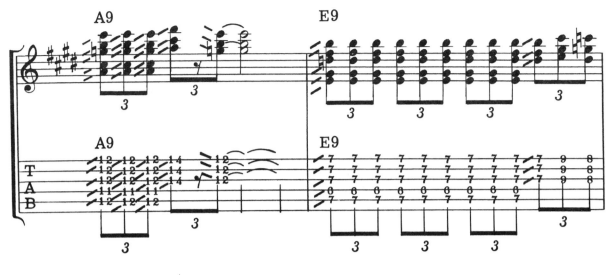

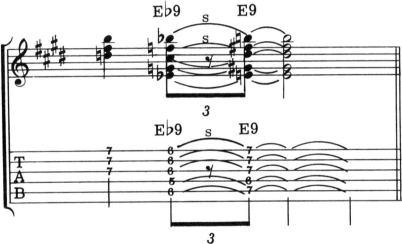

In more up-tempo Chicago blues formats such as the ever-present "Got My Mojo Workin'," the C9 chord is used even more rhythmically, with the combination sometimes of lead-in bass notes. The next piece illustrates this technique. This is also a very gospel-oriented "double time" rhythm lick, reminiscent of the rousing climaxes often heard at the end of gospel tunes.

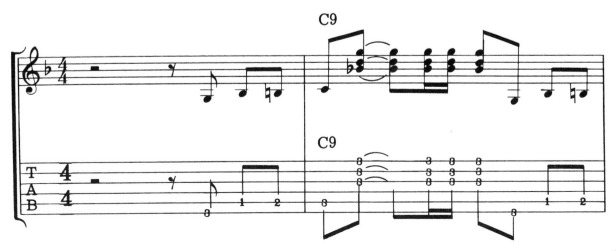

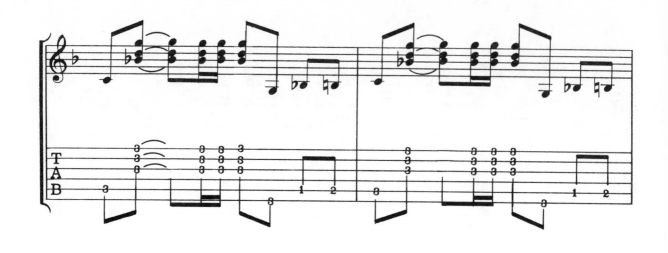

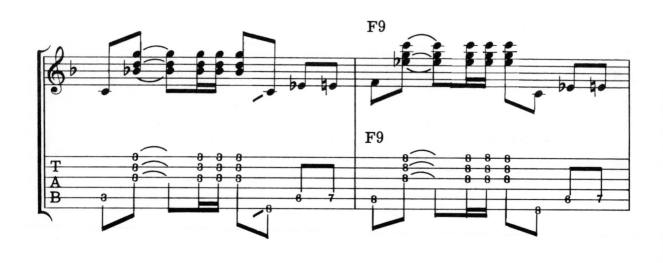

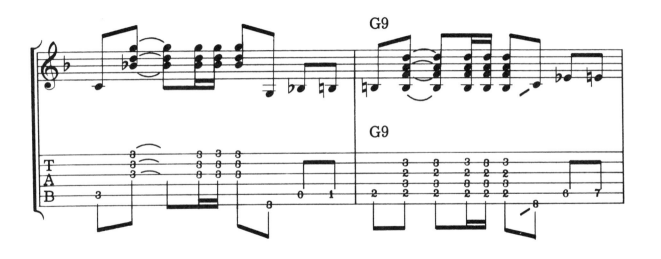

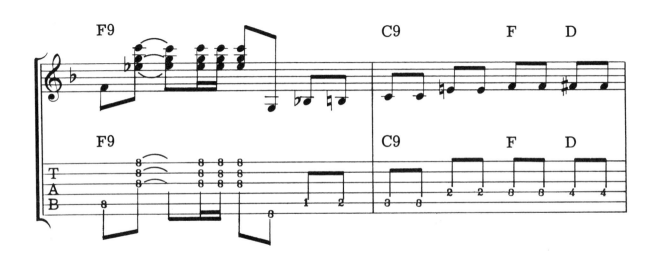

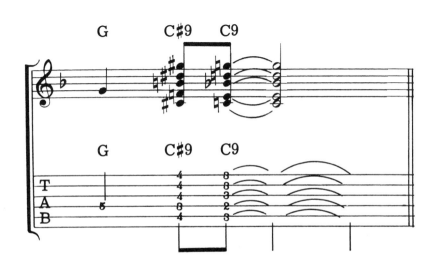

THE C9 CHORD POSITION IN "FUNK" GUITAR

The combination of single-note work and chords is even more prevalent in this form of rhythm-and-blues playing, and constitutes some of the most syncopated playing to be heard. The ability to rapidly change positions from single-note work to chords is crucial to this style, and in the exercises that follow we will see some of the possibilities.

In this first example, the bass lead-up notes must be followed rapidly by a succession of three very quick down-up-down strokes on the barred portion of the ninth chord:

The next little piece consists of three elements: first, the bass-note lead-in, secondly, the chord riff, and finally, a three-note slide "answer." Essentially we are taking the last exercise and adding one more distinct element to it.

This style is reminiscent of the playing of the great R&B guitarist Cornell Dupree, who can be heard on records by King Curtis, Stuff, and many others.

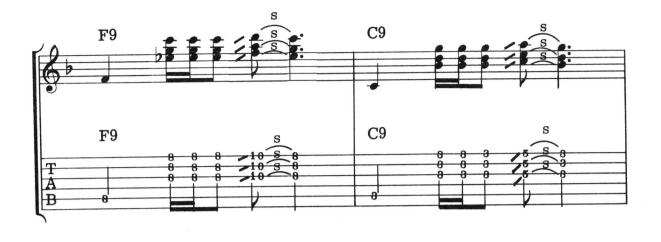

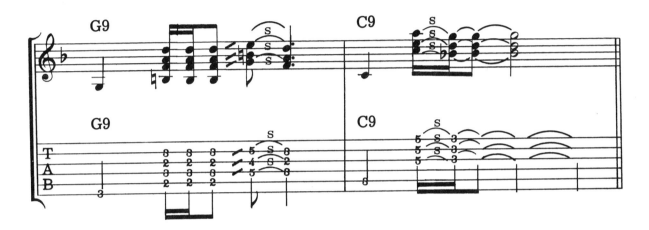

One of the most distinct features of Dupree's playing is his use of certain double-note runs in combination with the chord work. The following are a group of these licks to practice. They correspond to this C9 position of E that we've been working in, and since they use the G and high E strings, the B string must be damped out if you are using a flat pick only. The best way to achieve this important technique is by having one of the fingers that is actually fretting a note lightly *slide* along the middle unwanted string to cut out the vibration. Keep working at them until they sound really smooth.

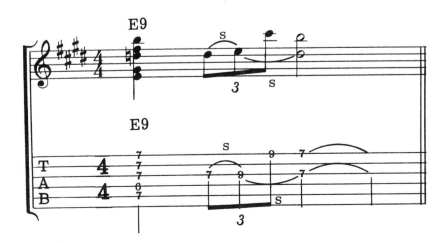

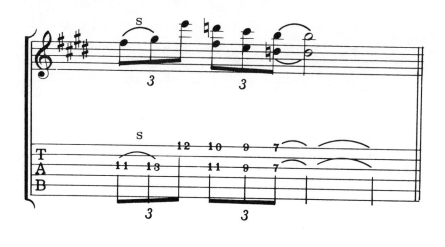

Here is a piece that puts it all together. It's based on Cornell Dupree's opening guitar lick in King Curtis' "Memphis Soul Stew," a song in which Curtis introduces each member of the band, with each player in turn answering with an opening lick. Note how it starts off with single-note work, but eventually develops into a complex interweaving of chordal and single-note acrobatics. Good luck with it, and keep damping!

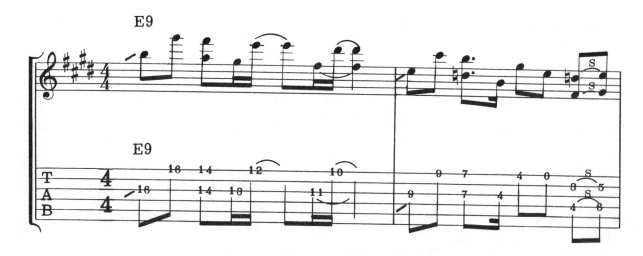

CONTEMPORARY ROCK RHYTHM GUITAR

No one can turn on the radio these days without being reminded that not only is rock becoming an increasingly rhythmic form of music, but that the guitar is, as always, at the very heart and soul of this pulse. The rhythm player in rock must act as the bridge between the bassist and the drummer. The term "lock-in" is one I often heard in my early days in the studio, and this task is best achieved by simply and truly *listening*. As exemplified in the playing of people like Peter Townshend, Jimi Hendrix, and the legions of heavy-metal guitarists, rock rhythm guitar can truly be just as emotional and spectacular as the more dominant, lead-guitar styles. "Power" chords aren't "power" chords for nothing, and in the sections that follow we'll explore the many as-

pects of rock rhythm guitar that make this such an important wealth of knowledge for any guitarist, no matter what his or her aspirations may be.

POWER CHORDS

I guess the term "power chords" began with the late sixties and early seventies form of rock music that cut its teeth on the psychedelic sound of the sixties groups. Long, loud, and with sustaining volume, groups like the Who, Led Zeppelin, and Grand Funk Railroad have utilized those power chords to their fullest. In the later seventies and early eighties the heavy-metal bands such as Van Halen, Iron Maiden, Black Sabbath, AC/DC, and Blue Öyster Cult have been flailing away in true power-chord tradition.

What probably gives power chords their

distinction is the fact that they are very often "modal" in nature. This means that there is rarely a major or minor third contained in the chord. Usually, these chords consist of the root and the fifth, often with one of the two doubled on a higher octave. This type of configuration, when played often, gives birth to certain abbreviated chord forms not necessarily used in other styles of guitar playing. The following group of photographs illustrates some of these partial chord forms.

The top photograph shows a partial form of open E, allowing the low E, B, and middle E notes to be sounded, while the index finger is lying across and damping out the top three strings.

The middle photo shows a similar situation for the open A-chord position. The index finger can be used to sound the D, G, and B strings also, as opposed to just two fretted strings. Remember to lightly touch the high E to damp that string.

The barre positions for the power chords, shown in the bottom photo, both in the E and A forms, are more adaptable to the damping situation, because the index finger, normally barring anyway, can now lightly lie across the top three strings, damping them out.

POWER-CHORD PROGRESSIONS

Over the years, certain progressions that seem to keep showing their faces in the hard-rock and power-chord songs would be great exercises for the aspiring power player. The following are a group that best represent archetypal power-chord progressions.

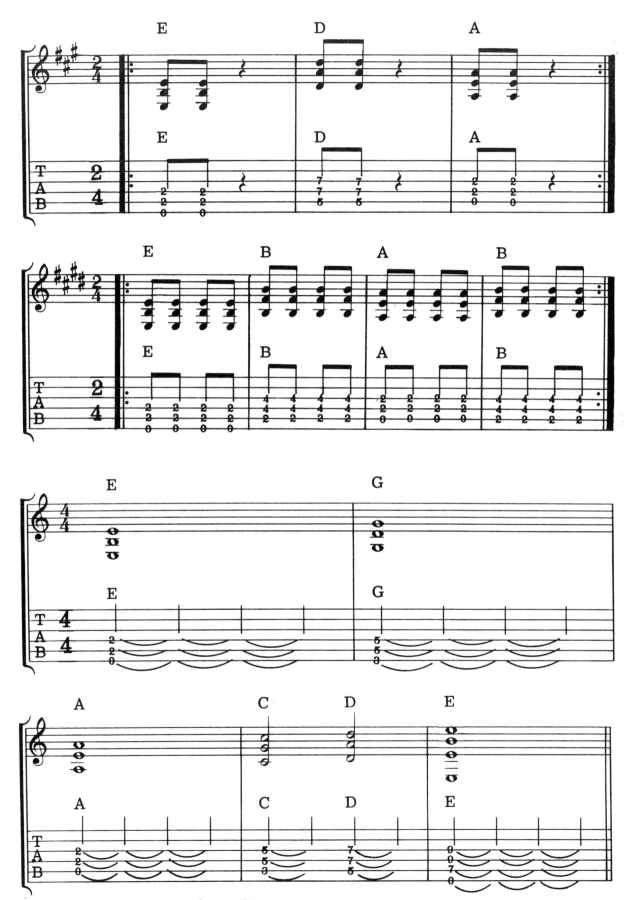

PERCUSSIVE DAMPING

On many of the "heaviest" guitar parts heard in hard rock, we often hear "chunka-chunkas" played between power chords. This is simply achieved by releasing the pressure of one of the fingers playing the power chord (in most cases, the index finger) and damping *all* the strings so your picking hand can then play across them and create that chunky sound. It's especially effective at high volumes, where this effect seems to "jump" out of the speakers! Here's a power-chord progression combined with this technique:

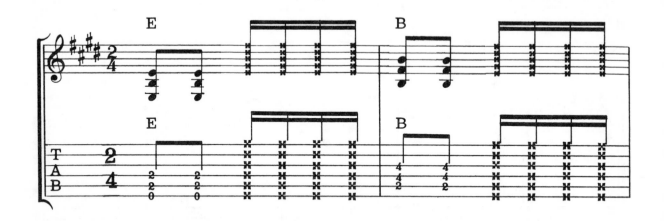

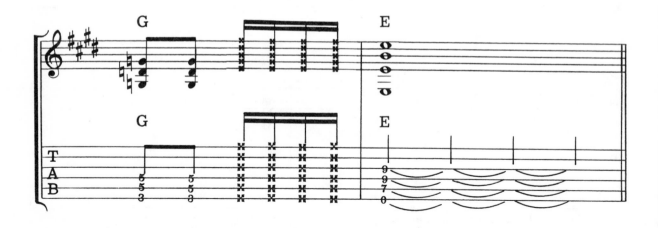

THE POWER-CHORD STYLE OF
JIMI HENDRIX

The great Jimi Hendrix was capable of a broad range of expressive guitar styles. Even his power-chord style was one of subtlety and finesse, exemplified in his use of combining bass notes and runs with power-chord answers. "Purple Haze," one of his early classics, utilized this guitar style and helped to set this song apart from many other "heavy" tunes being played during that same era. Here is an idealized version of the main guitar part of that song, which was used as an introduction and as backup for the verses.

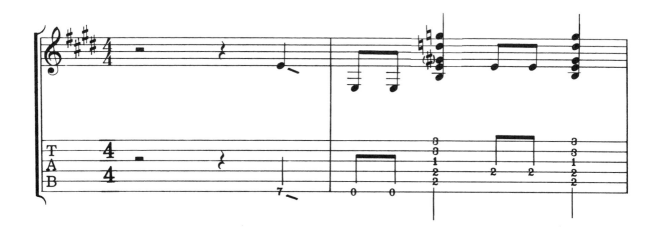

Here's another of Jimi's styles, reminiscent of the combined bass run and chord work discussed in the section on R&B guitar styles:

PETER TOWNSHEND—FLOURISHES AND SUSPENSIONS

Peter Townshend of the Who is a master innovator of many classic rock rhythm-guitar styles. Among his most identifiable traits are right-hand flourishes (often accompanied by leaps in the air), repetitive use of suspended fourth chords, and playing of power chords laced with constant bass patterns that keep the listener in constant anticipation of his next move. (We'll skip guitar smashing in this chapter!)

First, as an example of the right-hand flourishes, I've devised this exercise as a means of illustrating the use of this technique interwoven with a more conventional power-chord part:

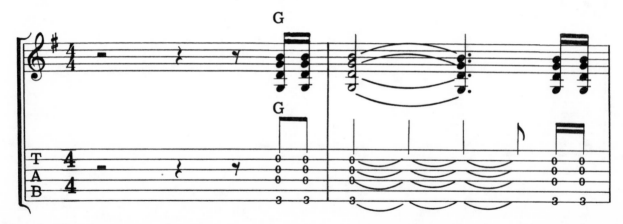

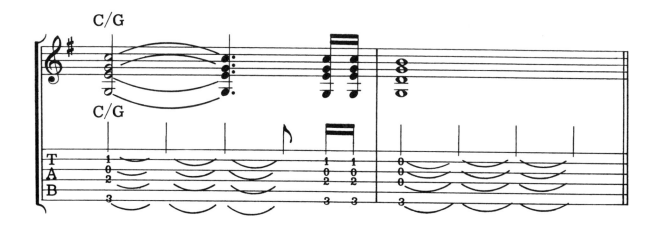

His use of suspended fourth chords, especially in combination with constant bass notes, is one of Townshend's most recognizable sounds. The Who's famous rock opera *Tommy* was a collection of music rich in this technique, with songs like "Pinball Wizard" having guitar parts based on this sound. The following piece illustrates this style:

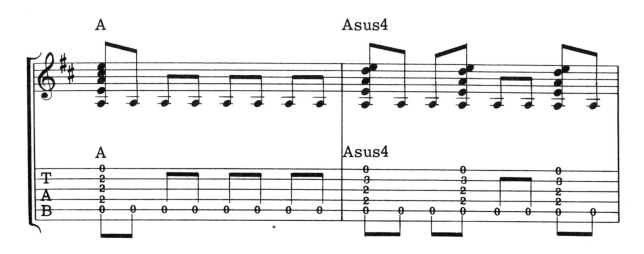

THE RHYTHMIC STYLE OF
KEITH RICHARDS

Keith Richards, the driving guitar force behind the Rolling Stones since their beginning, boasts a rhythmic style that, while Chuck Berry-influenced, has become his own distinct sound. The chord structures most preferred by Keith usually take the open-G or the barred-A form, and he uses the partial-C form hammer-ons over them to create a suspended-chord feeling. This position so resembles the open-G tuning positions that occur on the top five strings that Richards many times uses open-G tuning for these rhythm parts, often on a guitar strung with only five strings!

This first exercise resembles his intro to "Brown Sugar," and illustrates the power-chord possibilities that can be found within these partial-barre forms.

3

Playing Electric Lead Guitar

When you think of the electric guitar, the term "lead guitar" is probably the first that comes to mind. The lead guitarist is a hero of sorts—often the instrumental focal point in most of the music that falls under the categories of rock, country, blues, and rockabilly, as well as the evergrowing use of lead guitar in fusion music and modern jazz. The lead guitarist must often assume the role of responsibility dictated by his title, by leading the band. This is often because the lead player is many times the creative force behind what the band is playing in the first place; often he or she may be the writer of the music or the main focal point of the band when performing live. All of this makes lead guitar a physically and emotionally demanding medium, but of course, the rewards are great.

Lead guitar is one of the more eclectic forms of music making. A firm foundation in rhythm-guitar techniques is advisable to any aspiring lead player, no matter how much he or she desires to go head first into learning all those flashy licks. That is why we took an in-depth look into rhythm styles before embarking on this chapter.

The art form we call lead guitar is a broad, fascinating study, and in this chapter we'll delve into many of those great trade secrets, including string bending, hammer-ons, pull-offs, moving swiftly from one position to another, and the most widely used scale positions in lead guitar. Finally, we'll be taking a look at some demanding exercises designed to involve the many intricacies of lead-guitar playing. This is just the beginning, though, for after you've worked on this chapter, we'll start to "specialize" in various forms of lead guitar, such as Nashville styles, slide guitar, rockabilly, and rock. Now on with our playing!

The Blues and Rock Styles

Much of the lead playing heard in the contemporary rock world owes its beginnings to the earlier blues styles. Rock stars like Jimmy Page, Eric Clapton, and Jeff Beck learned from listening to such players as Buddy Guy, Otis Rush, Elmore James, and B.B. King. There was a period during the late sixties when guitarists like Mike Bloomfield, Danny Kalb, and Eric Clapton were educating us to a whole medium and group of musicians of whom we were all too unaware. I became a part of a blues craze that swept through my high school in New York. My friends and I hungrily gathered blues licks and songs; the jam sessions started when the school day ended. My knowledge of lead guitar began to take shape. I pieced solos and riffs together, and

developed an understanding of the fingerboard that enabled me to start "talking" on the guitar.

To further understand the concept of building knowledge on the fingerboard, I've divided the scales you'll be learning into groups, depending on the overall movement between positions that the particular scale may require.

BLUES/ROCK PATTERN NO. 1

This pattern, in the "open" position of E, is the most basic yet often used scale in blues and rock improvisation. Try playing it here in the alternating-pick style: down, up, down, up, etc. (See also Diagram 6 at right.)

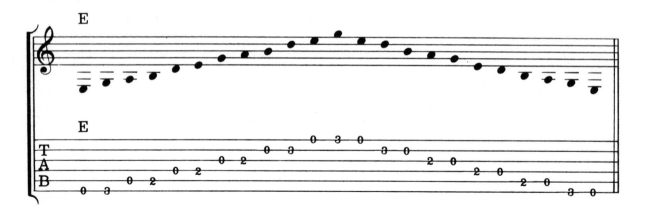

This next scale is basically the same pattern, only now played in a "closed" position. It's for the key of G, and you should take note of the use of the Bb on the A string played by the

index finger, rather than making an exact mirror of the open-E position by playing the Bb on the sixth fret of the low E string. (See also Diagram 7 at right.)

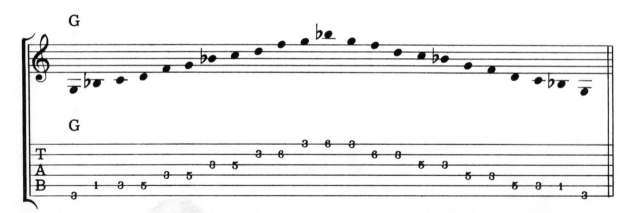

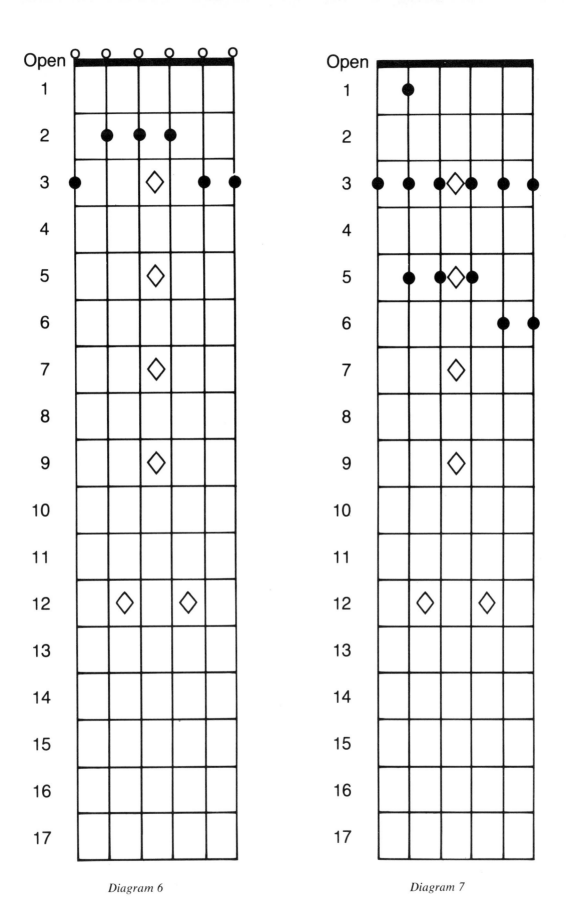

Diagram 6

Diagram 7

PASSING NOTES

The two scale positions we've just looked at are of course the basis of much lead improvisation. There are certain notes, however, that, while not actually played in those scales, were *implied* by the movement of the notes that skipped over them. These special notes are called "passing" notes, and are often responsible for that "blue" note sound heard when the techniques of string bending, slide, and other specialties are used. Applications of passing notes will be covered in later pages, but first here are the same two scales, with these blue "passing" notes added. The new notes are circled for easier identification.

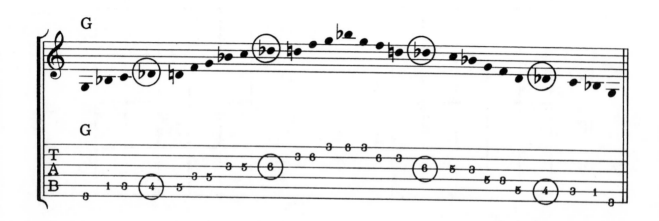

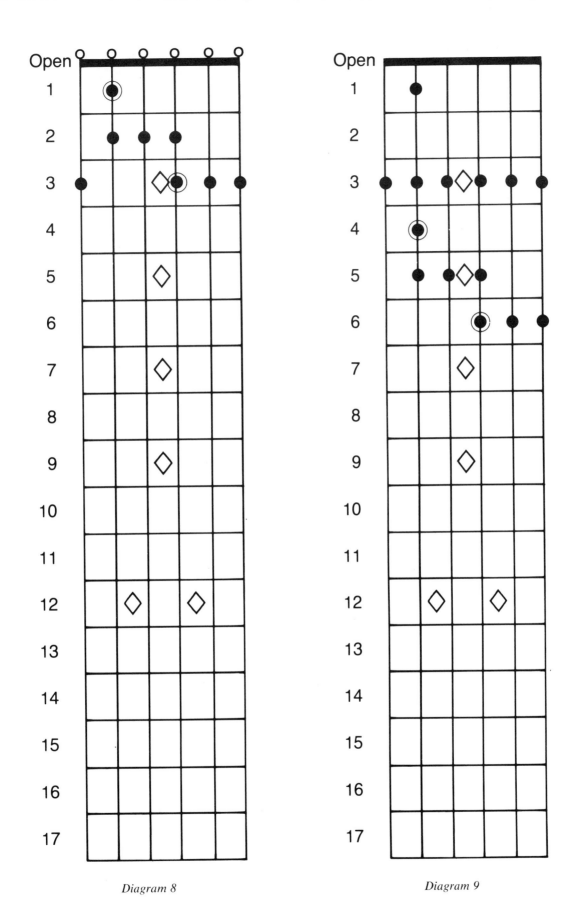

Diagram 8

Diagram 9

53

LICKS—BLUES/ROCK PATTERN NO. 1

I'm sure that while practicing the last two passing-note positions, you couldn't help but hear echoes of past licks. Well, here come the licks. This group is designed to help you get the most out of the first patterns and passing-note scales we've just covered. Please try to see just where the passing notes are and listen to the kind of new sounds they create.

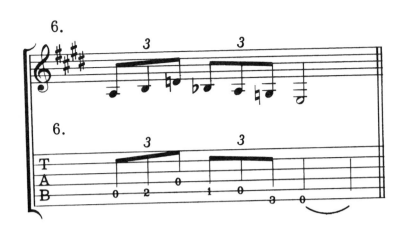

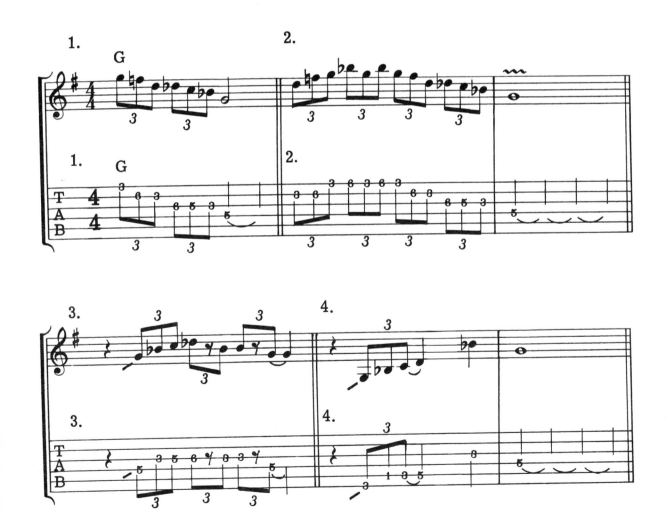

55

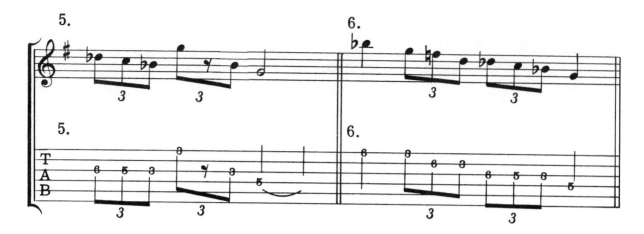

BLUES/ROCK PATTERN NO. 2

This pattern simply takes the past scales and adds a new, second position to them, which lends itself to even further improvisational properties. The changing of positions brings to light an exciting technique: that of "sliding" between notes to enter a new position or to return back to the old one. "Sliding" creates an endless supply of new licks and ideas as well, because of its expressive qualities.

Here are the two open and closed patterns using slides to help get you into the new, higher positions. The slides should occur with the same finger that is playing the note on which you begin the slide. This is one of the ways of completely shifting positions. The slides, by the way, also imply the passing notes we've been talking about. Be sure to practice them going both up *and* down, as I've indicated in the music. This will give you a better picture of the versatility of this sliding technique for getting to and from various positions.

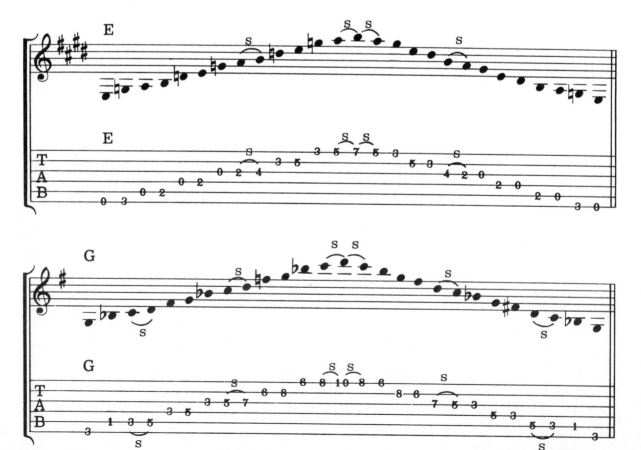

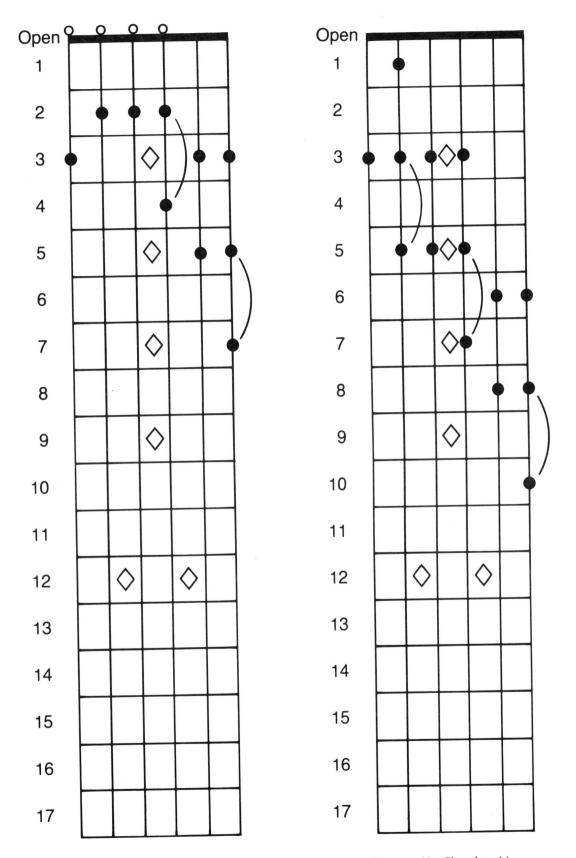

Diagram 10   Open position   *Diagram 11   Closed position*

the added flexibility of using slides between notes. You'll see that at times it's advantageous to give each note in a sliding situation its own time value, whereas we'll sometimes just slide *directly* to the note, from a more indiscriminate point below or above it.

The following collection of licks explore a great deal of what is available to the lead guitarist within these new scale positions and with

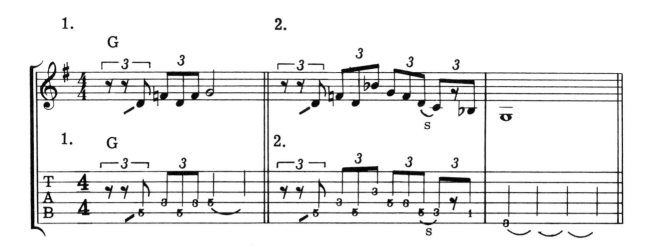

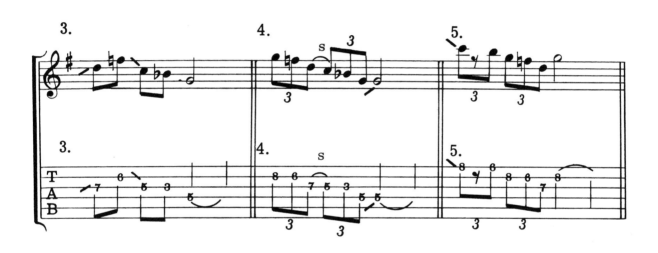

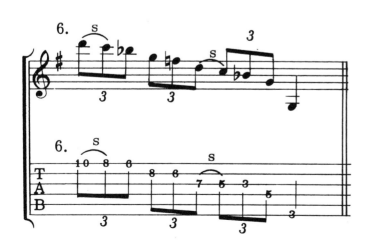

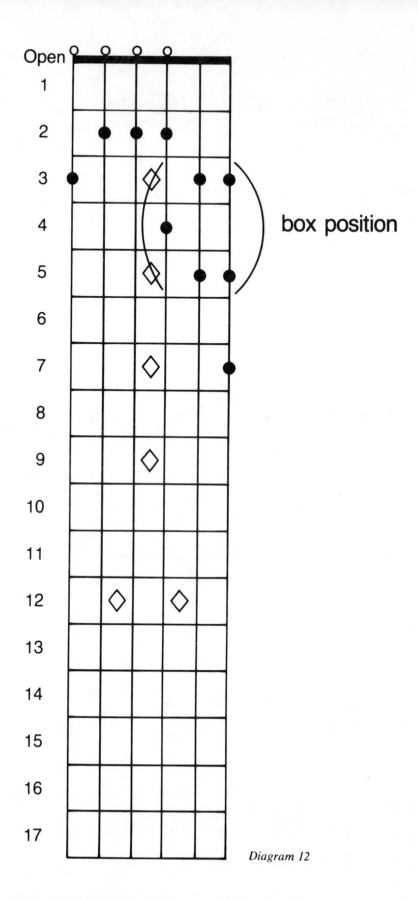

box position

Diagram 12

HIGH END "BOX" POSITIONS

One position I've gotten much mileage out of over the years is an integral part of the scale with which we've just been working. I call it a box position, because it creates a wealth of lead guitar possibilities within relatively close confines. You'll understand what I mean if you study the following scale and Diagram 12 and see where I've indicated the box:

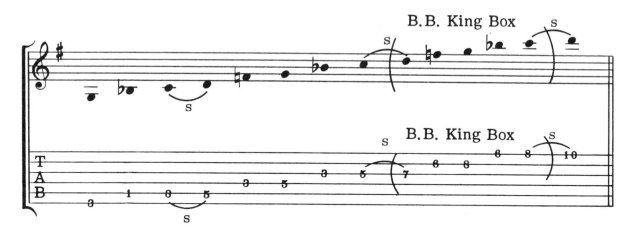

This exercise is designed to develop rapid picking within the close quarters of a position such as this box. Try to play it faster and faster as you become more relaxed with it.

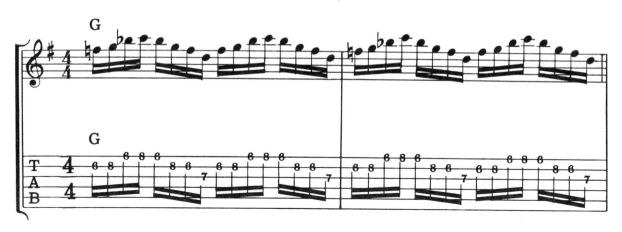

Here are a group of licks I've selected to combine the properties of the box position with the other techniques we've been discussing.

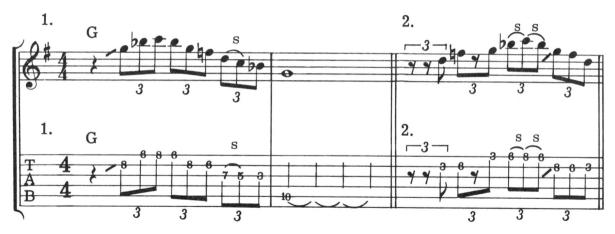

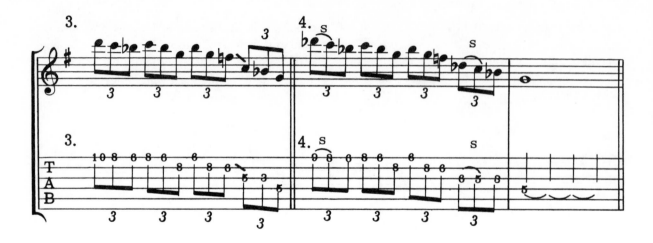

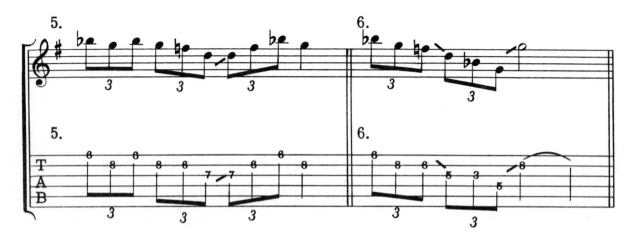

BLUES/ROCK PATTERN NO. 3

This pattern is really a higher *position* than the previous two; its lowest note begins on the **A string**, as opposed to the usual low **E.** You'll see that it contains the same note relationships as all blues scales and that it flows from one position to the other just as blues pattern no. 2 did. To illustrate where this position is in relation to its first position, I've written it out here for the third position of the key of **E.** (See also Diagram 13.)

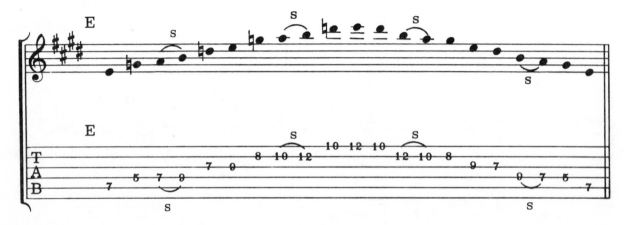

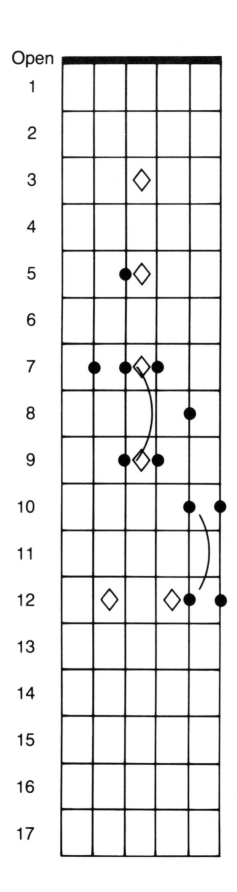

Diagram 13

This scale shows you where to find the
bluesy, passing notes within this position.

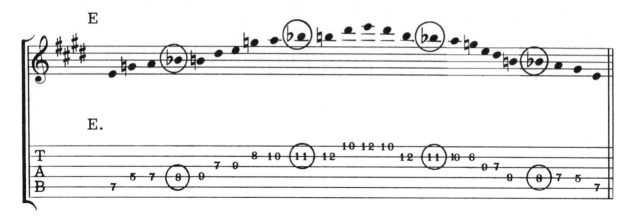

LICKS—BLUES/ROCK PATTERN NO. 3

Using the same techniques we applied to
the other exercises, this collection of licks will
help you to develop a better feel for what's
available to you in this new, higher position.

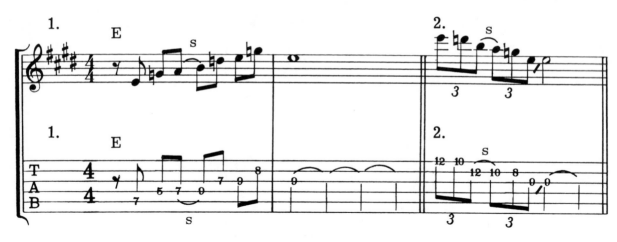

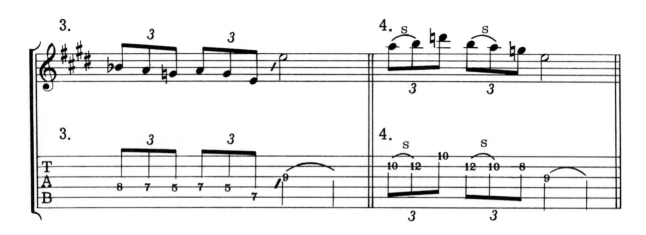

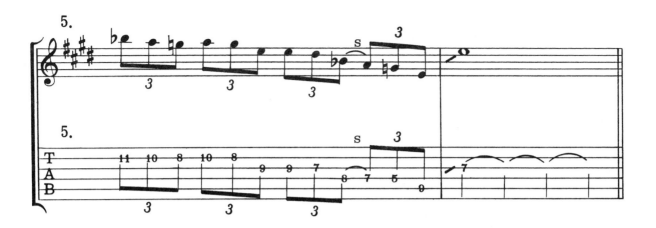

HAMMER-ONS AND PULL-OFFS

These two techniques, while possessing rather unusual titles, are among *the* most important tools a lead guitarist can ever acquire. As with the use of slides, these techniques help to give new life to the string itself, keeping it vibrating without having to actually pick the string again. Through the use of hammer-ons and pull-offs, you can improve to the point where you can be picking only one out of five notes during a long flourish of runs! Indeed, this is how flashy players can play with one hand: through a strong development of left-hand *pull-offs* and *hammer-ons*.

THE HAMMER-ON

In this technique we do just as the name says: we actually "hammer" a new note on top of the old one, getting the new one to ring just as true as the first (picked) note did. One of the most common misconceptions regarding hammer-ons is that students feel they must begin the hammer-on with their hammering finger high above the fingerboard. In fact, the *closer* you are, and the harder you can hammer within close range, the better off and more accurate you'll be.

For this first simple illustration of a hammer-on involving the third fret on the high E string, and the hammer-on to the sixth fret with your third finger, the following photo shows the proper pre-hammering position and angle of my hand. Notice how my hand is slightly angled so the palm is turned toward the guitar itself:

on would only create a nearly silent situation. Here's the *pull-off* with a photo illustrating the proper position just after the "pluck" has occurred:

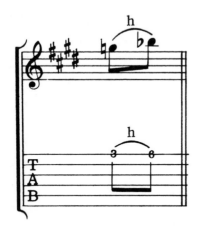

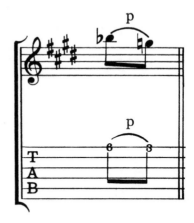

THE PULL-OFF

This technique is not the exact reversal of hammering-on, as some people might think; rather, it is a downward left-hand "pluck," which is used to actually give the string new life. A "lift-off" merely reversing the hammer-

In these next two scales, you'll start to see how using these techniques can actually make a simple blues scale start to sound as though you're really playing. Keep in mind how you must always keep that first finger moving from string to string in the closed position, always ready for the pull-off to occur:

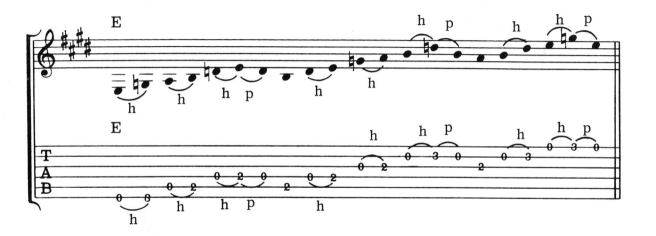

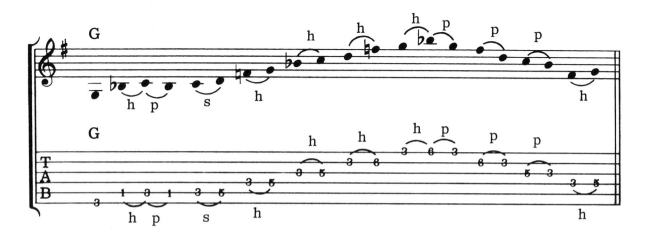

THE "BACKTRACK" SCALE

This exercise starts to really put it all together. You must combine hammers and pulls; then only pulls; and keep your fingers moving while many strings are played, and then played *again* as a new part of the phrase. Hence, the "backtrack" name. Here again, you should learn it both for the open position of E and the closed position of G. Try to get to the point where you can play them **fast**.

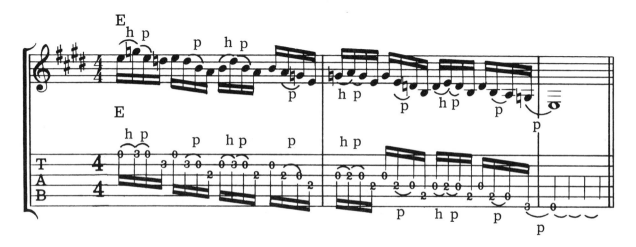

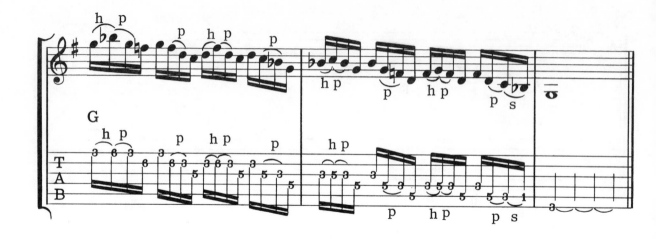

LICKS WITH HAMMER-ONS AND PULL-OFFS

I've divided this next assemblage of licks and runs into the three blues/rock scale positions we've been working with so far. Each position has its own properties that lend **themselves** to improvisational ideas that may not be found in other positions. Have fun with them, and try to experiment with any new **ideas that might come to mind.** *Please!*

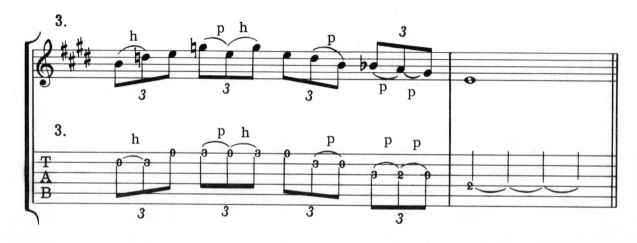

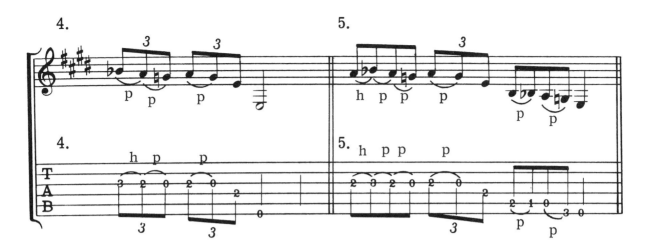

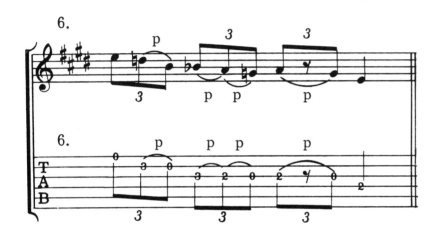

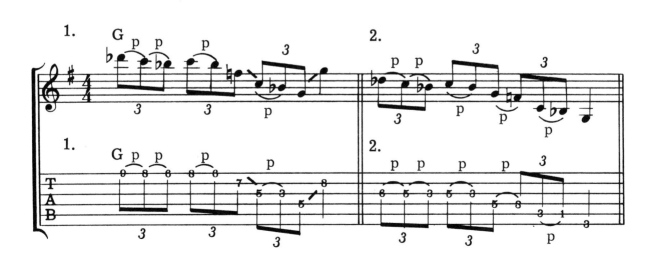

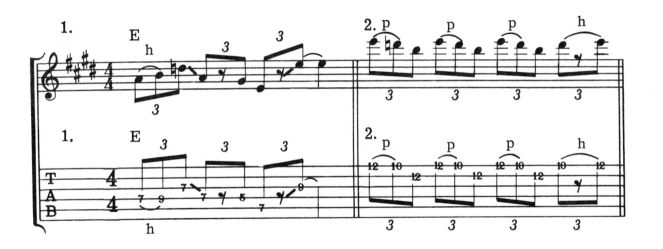

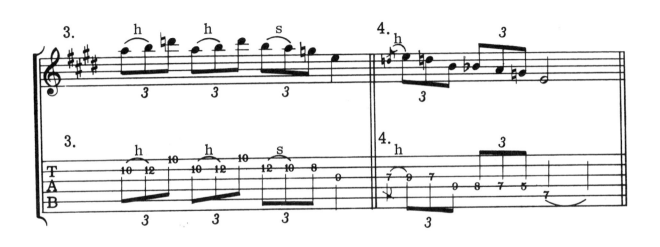

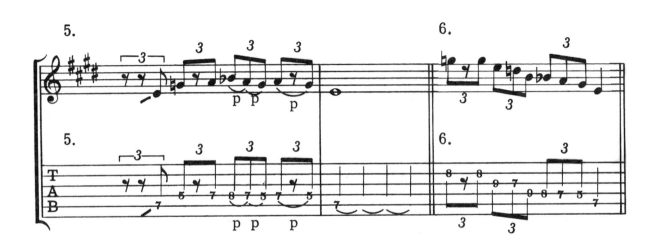

The Art of String Bending

Now that we've covered some of the most useful tools the lead guitarist must have, it's time to go on to what I consider the ultimate means of expression in the lead player's vocabulary: the fine art of string bending.

Since I feel string bending is such an important part of guitar playing, I want to help clear up many of the potential problems I've encountered while teaching it. First, your strings, as stated earlier, should be no lighter than a set that has the gauge of .010 for the high E string (and the G string *must* be of the unwound variety if you expect to get the most bending power out of your guitar).

There are two types of bends: toward you, and away from you. The physical means of achieving these bends are often the most misunderstood techniques in lead guitar playing. Remember, *other* fingers should always be used (if available) to help bend on the same string *behind* the actual note that's being bent. This photo illustrates what I mean. It shows a bend *toward* you; note how my first two fingers are helping the third finger to reach the note we are bending to.

PIVOTING

The other characteristic crucial to string bending, and the most commonly overlooked, is that when you are bending *away* from you, a *pivoting* motion used by your left hand combined with the actual bend is what is needed to ensure the proper strength required to create the bend.

This "pivot," a technique I'll be referring to many times over in this book, is achieved by resting the bone just below the index finger against the side of the neck. It is from this point that the pivot occurs. This enables you to have more leverage when bending away, and keeps the fingers in a consistent position compared to the curled-under look that happens when you bend improperly. These three photos tell the story. The first one shows the three-fingered bend held incorrectly, complete with the uncomfortable curl that occurs with the fingers.

Here is the proper way to bend, with the pivoting leverage easing the strain:

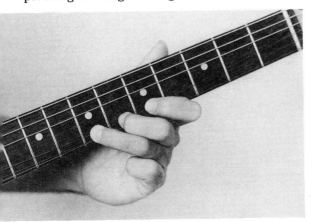

One-finger bends, almost **always** done with the index finger, are also popular in rock and blues; the same pivoting motion should be called on to aid in the playing of these positions:

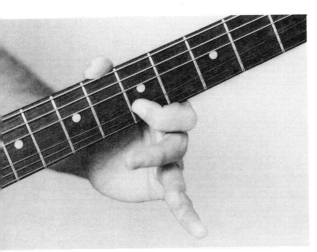

WHAT NOTES ARE BENT?

Let's go back and take a look at all the blues/rock positions we've been discussing, and see just what notes are bent most often. Before we do, though, here's a clue that will help you locate these bending notes for yourself. As you've probably noticed already, the blues/rock scale consists mainly of five notes: *root, minor third, fourth, fifth,* and *seventh,* then on to a second, *higher octave of the root,* always in this same order. If you bend the minor third up one half step, you'll reach a *major* **third,** defining the chord you're playing against as a major chord. You also have the option to bend this note up a *whole* step, reaching the *fourth.* The next note you can bend actually *is* the fourth, and this is where most of the bluesy bends lie, because you have the option of bending one fret to the "blue" flatted fifth, or all the way up to the regular fifth by bending it a whole step. The last note you may bend is the seventh. This is a tantalizing whole step below the root and is almost always bent up right to that root note. Of course, these notes repeat themselves again in any one of these blues/rock scales, and sometimes the bends may be possible in only *one* of the places where the right note occurs.

This idiosyncracy occurs in the following first blues scale, where the use of certain open notes makes bending impossible until you reach the same notes in a higher position. The notes that are circled are the ones to bend:

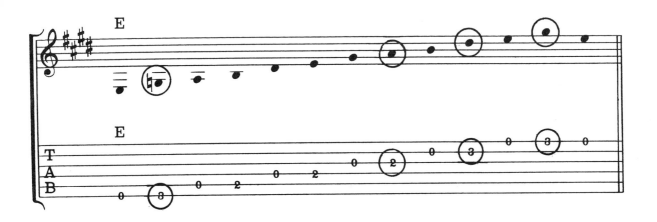

This position no. 2, going higher up the fingerboard, brings about more bending possibilities. Here again, the circled notes are the ones most often bent:

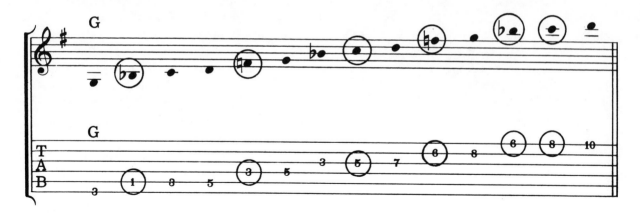

Here is the closed position of this pattern in E. Note how being closed brings about more bending possibilities in the lower register:

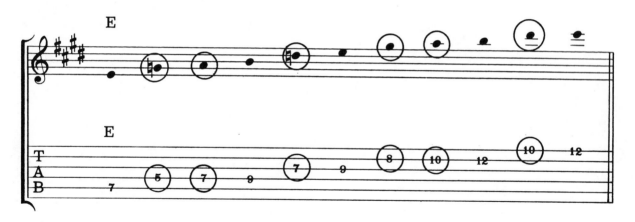

STRING BENDING AS SUBSTITUTION

It is essential to your success as a player who uses string bending to have firm control and understanding of this technique. Often I hear the groping wails of a lead guitarist who really has *no* idea what he's bending to or for what reason he's bending in the first place! The first thing to remember is that this technique is *musical*, and a deeper knowledge of what is harmonically going on when you bend a string is invaluable to your success. For this reason, I've chosen to introduce you to string-bending licks as *substitutions* for the techniques we've already discussed: slides, hammer-ons, and pull-offs. This way you'll see how important it is to know just what note you want to reach with a bend. After all, this is one technique where the note exists entirely in your hands. *You* control the pitch.

For starters, here are a group of runs from the open-E blues/rock positions. The first lick is with the previous techniques, while the second uses bends to substitute for some part of it. Remember, even if it makes you lose a little time at first, always help the bend with as many available fingers as you have below the finger that's actually playing the note:

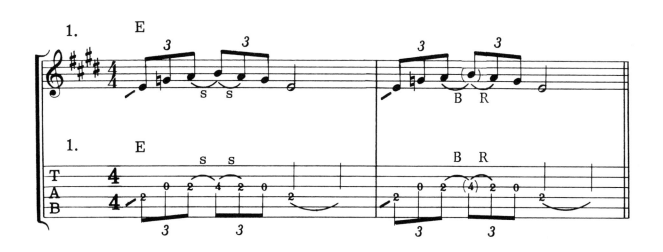

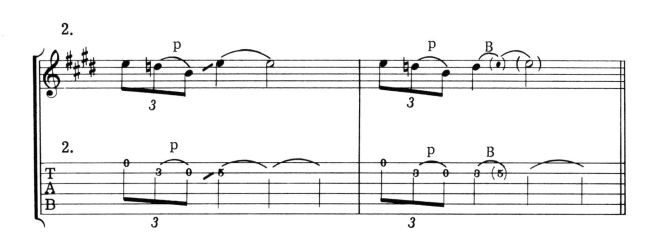

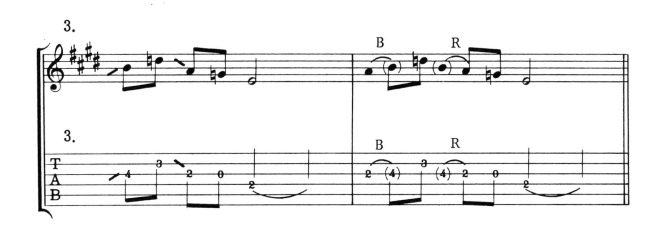

In this exercise, you'll notice the utilization of certain stemless notes: that is to say that there are some notes with no time value. This simply means that the notes are bent up to *immediately*, rather than giving separate time values to both the unbent *and* the bent notes, as we've been doing so far.

Here are a group of bend substitutions for the G closed position:

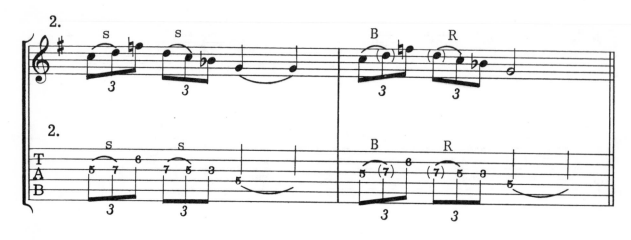

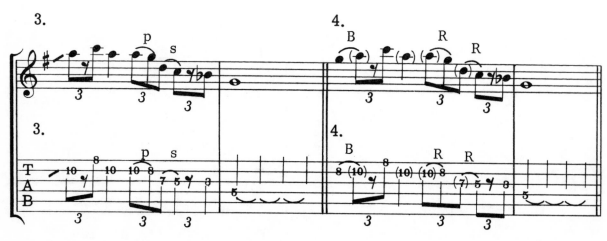

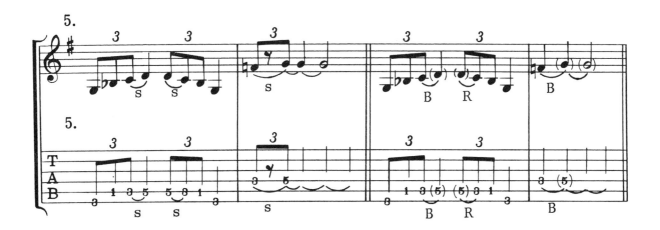

One of the most popular applications of string bending in blues is the trick of bending up to a note and then sounding that same note in its standard, fretted position. This is a very good way to practice and develop your control over just how far you should bend the strings. The licks that follow are prime examples of this style.

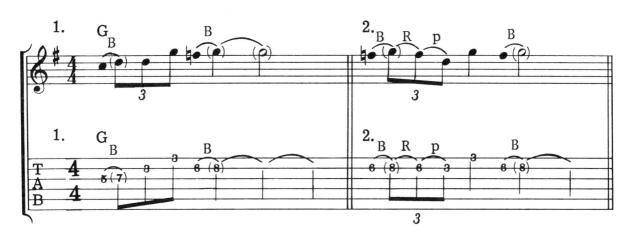

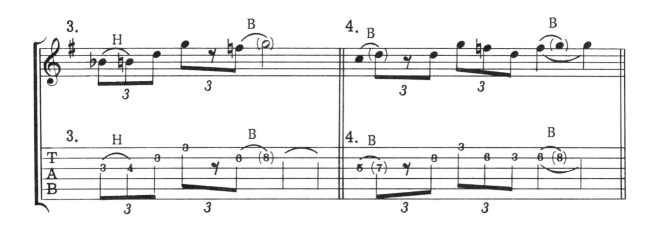

HAVING THE NOTE BENT
BEFORE RELEASE

Creating a "silent" bend, that is, having the note already bent up to the desired pitch before releasing it, is where you really separate the men from the boys as far as string bending is concerned. What is required, in essence, is enough experience at string bending that you already have the *feel* of how far a note must be bent, right in your fingertips. The creative benefits of this knowledge are endless, and you develop a much greater awareness of the potentials within your grasp.

The next group of licks are designed to develop this technique. Try to get up to the bent notes really silently before you actually sound them. If you don't quite get it the first time, keep trying until you begin to have an idea beforehand about how far you must bend it.

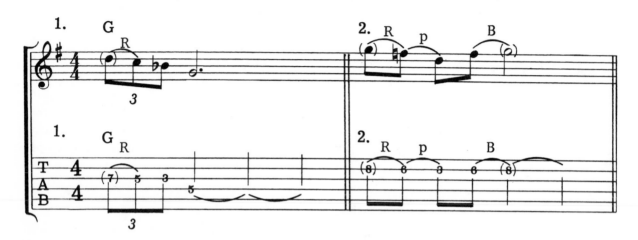

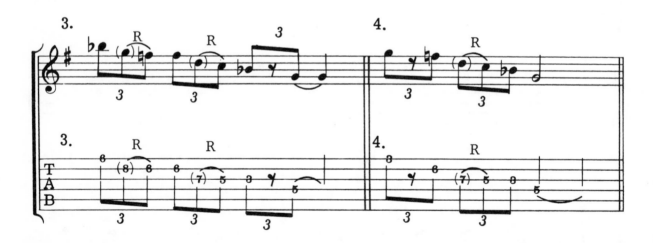

STARTING TO COMBINE THE TECHNIQUES

It is when you start to combine the techniques of string bending, sliding, hammer-ons, and pull-offs that you really start to "talk." Often a bend, release, and pull-off may occur before another note is actually picked. This is where real string control comes in, and you must have confidence in your technique, to make it work.

I've chosen the next group of exercises as a means of helping you to see the various combimations that can occur in lead playing. These are some of my favorite runs; they constitute some pretty advanced playing. Again, pay close attention to just what techniques are being called on, and don't be satisfied until it sounds right to you.

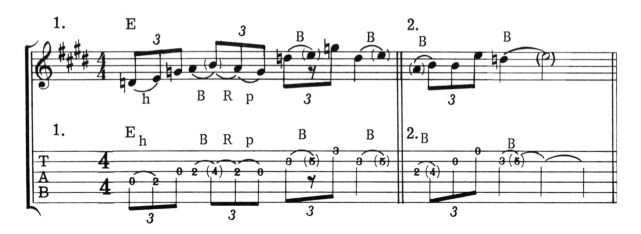

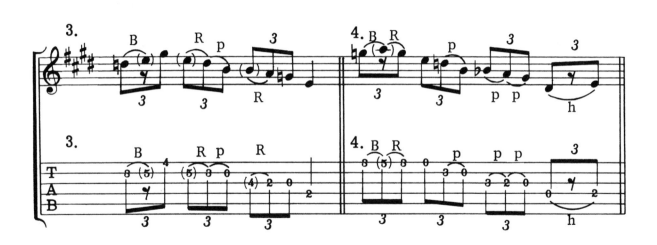

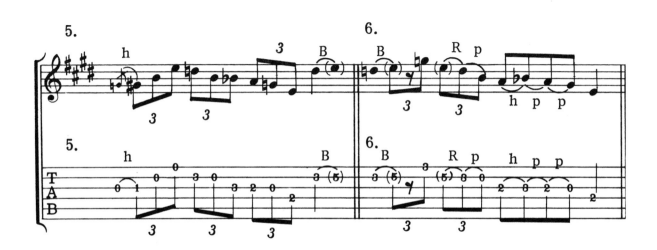

80

VIBRATO

Since we're starting to get into more difficult material combining many techniques, let's take a brief detour here to discuss the makeup of proper vibrato.

It's important to keep in mind that vibrato is used to help a note *sustain* longer through the added vibration you are giving the string. There are many types of vibrato, especially in terms of variances in vibration, but there is only one right way of achieving this sound!

One problem most encountered by someone new to vibrato playing is the tendency to overwork to achieve the vibrato. The technique I *completely* recommend is using a hand position just like the one described in the section on bending a string *away* from you. This way, you'll be able to use that same gear-like pivoting motion to create the vibrato. The mistake many players make is to not have the fretting hand anchored anywhere, thereby putting all the responsibility on the fingers and the forearm, and making it a more difficult sound to control.

Anyone who's ever watched B.B. King play can't help but notice his marvelous one-finger vibrato technique. Imitating him in my early years was what turned me on to this type of vibrato, and I wanted that same freedom of motion he gets when he starts to achieve that "butterfly" appearance from his hand moving so rapidly.

The next two photographs illustrate the proper positions in the pull and return stages of this pivoting vibrato. First, start without the string bent, then pivot from the bone just below your index finger. This pivot will *naturally* pull the string just far enough to vibrate it while not drastically changing its pitch. Observe how no other part of the hand is really holding on to the neck except for the pivoting point and the fretting finger. You should also try to raise your other fingers in the air, creating the "butterfly" that helps give the vibrato more momentum:

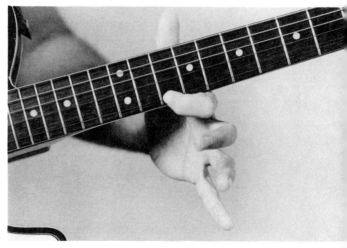

Just as in bending, it's good to have other fingers help out if the vibrato note is being played by the second, third, or fourth finger. You're still pivoting from the same spot, but now you have other fingers right on the same string helping to *distribute* the point at which the vibrato does occur. Here is a photo of how a vibrato played by the third finger should look. Take note of the positions of my other two fingers behind it:

BENDING WITH VIBRATO

Another tool for the lead guitarist, bends combined with vibrato, comprises some of the most expressive sounds in guitar playing. If you want to vibrate the string when it's bent *away* from you, the same *pivoting* rules apply. This photograph shows the proper position:

However, if you must bend *toward* you, you must use a completely new position in order to achieve a similar vibrato sound. In this case, the bend goes up, your thumb comes over the fingerboard (becoming in essence the *new* pivoting point), and the fingers and the back of the hand must spend more energy. This technique requires more control than the previous

one, so don't be discouraged if it gives you a hard time at first. Here's how it should look:

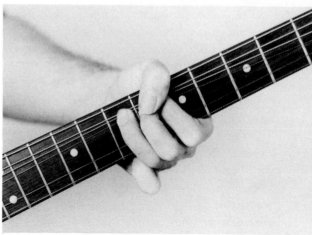

SOME "FLASH" LICKS

Let's face it; much of what we all *love* about lead guitar are some of the things that fall into the category of being "flashy"! All this really means is that a smooth combination of techniques is taking place, often in a repetitive fashion. I've never missed the opportunity to utilize some of this flash, yet I insist on it always being flashy in a musical sense as well as a physical sense.

The next group of licks constitute some of the more acrobatic positions I enjoy playing, and they combine all the techniques we've been working with so far, including bending combined with vibrato. Have fun!

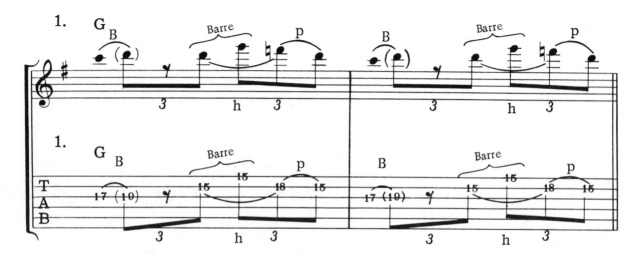

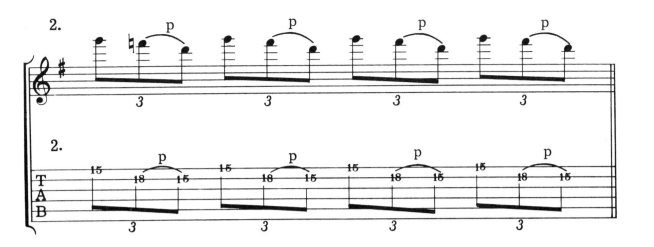

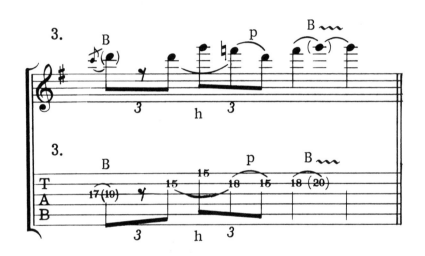

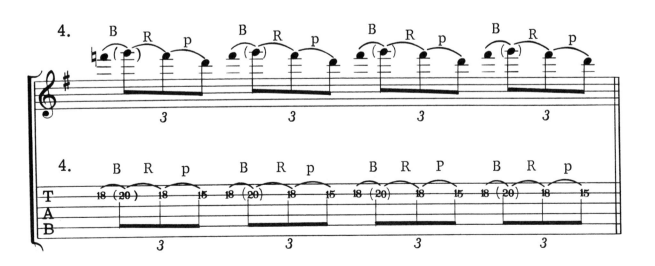

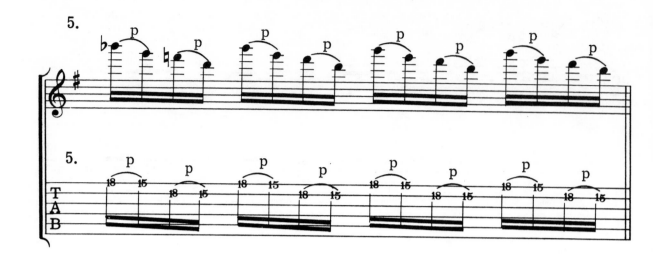

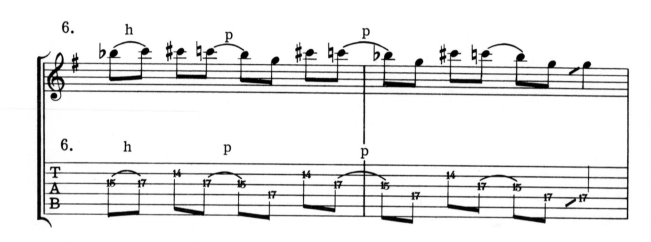

The Pentatonic Scales

Now that you've gotten well involved in lead-guitar styles and techniques, I feel it's important to get into another well of musical ideas used so often by lead guitarists: the major pentatonic scales. So far, we've been mainly concerned with the often discordant pentatonic (5-note) blues scales and the various techniques that can be applied to them. The primary difference in these pentatonic scales is that they are far more *major* in tonality than the blues scales, and in fact, contain *only* notes that can be found in the major scale. It is for this reason that many refer to these scales as "country" instead of "blues," even though the applications of the pentatonic scales are musically universal. In lead playing in particular, it is the ability to make smooth transitions be-

tween blues and pentatonic that enables you to create subtle changes in both emotional and musical content. Toward the end of this section, we'll take a look at some of these transitions in the context of full-fledged solos.

As in the section on the blues/rock scales, let's break the pentatonics down into three distinct positions.

PENTATONIC POSITION NO. 1

This scale, just like blues scale no. 1, is illustrated in an open position for the key of E. Take note of the much wider area of the fingerboard it spans, and how it literally ignores all the blues notes we've just gotten so used to playing: (See also Diagram 14, next page.)

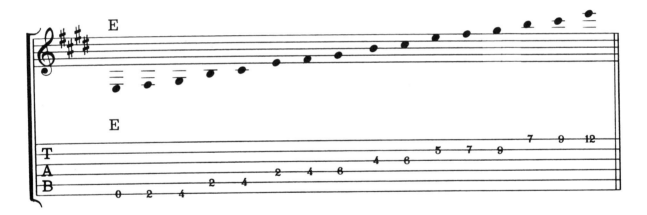

Here is exactly the same pentatonic scale, only now in a "closed" position for the key of G: (See also Diagram 15, next page.)

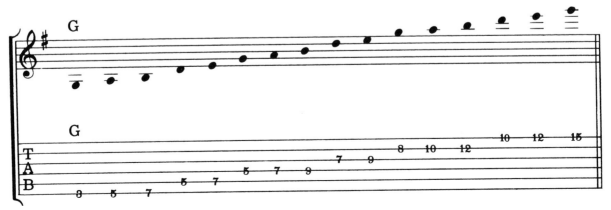

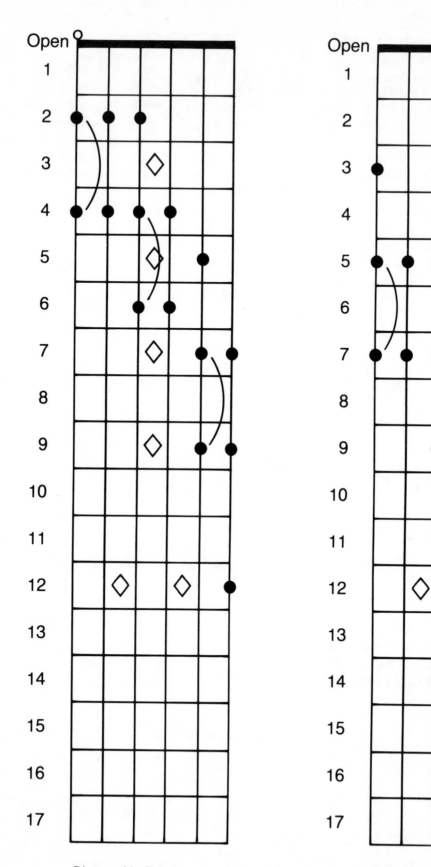

Diagram 14   E major

Diagram 15   G major

PASSING NOTES

There are passing notes that are used in improvising with these scales, just as in the blues positions; however, in the blues they were always *flatted fifths,* while in the pentatonic scales they play the role of the *flatted,* or *minor, thirds.*

Here again are the two open and closed positions, only this time with the addition of the passing notes in circles:

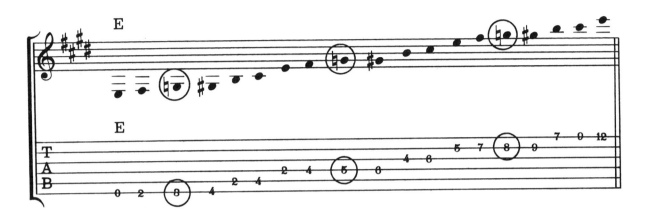

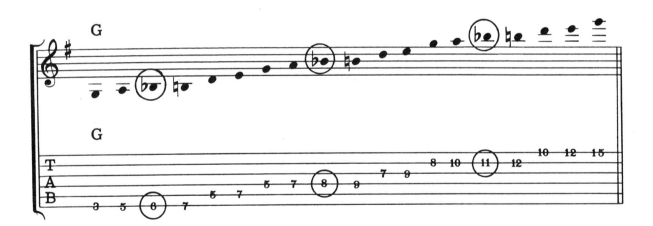

Just as we found in the case of the blues scales, the passing notes are those notes that are so often incorporated when a bend occurs. They can actually *be* the note you are bending to, or one of the notes you pass on the way to reaching the climax of the bend. This situation usually implies both half-step and whole-step bends. To illustrate the usual places where bends occur, here are the open and closed pentatonic scales again, only this time with the notes to be bent circled. Try some experimentation on your own and see how single-note and double-note bends sound at the different locations.

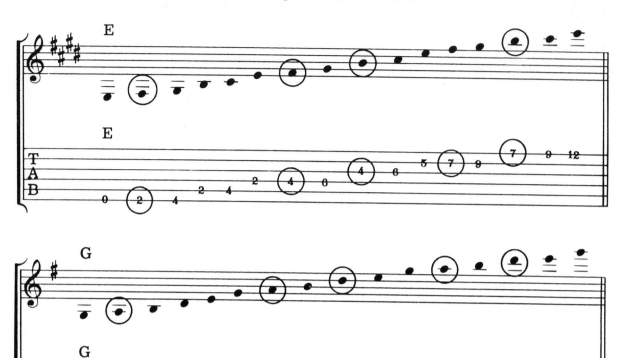

As you can see, the use of single-fret bends in a pentatonic situation creates "blue" notes once again. The knowledge that you have control over these kinds of notes is powerful, and can be put to great expressive as well as musical use. For example, if we were to play only half-step bends, reaching the *minor* thirds, we could be playing a "blue" note against the root chord, or the *seventh* of the IV chord! This is an exciting facet of lead playing we'll get more into when we cover the B.B. King pentatonic style; but first, here are a group of licks designed with single-note bends in mind. See how they sound against the tonic chord, and how they seem to take on a different identity against the IV chord. Remember to always use *other* fingers to help bend the strings.

89

Now, for the same exact scale positions, I have an entire group of whole-step-bend licks that involve bending to the *major* third of the tonic chord, creating a much more *resolved* sound.

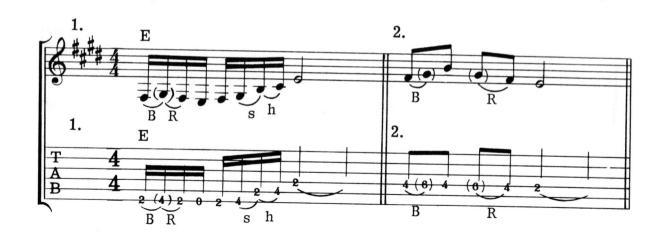

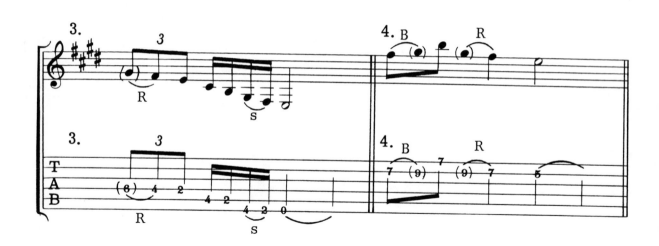

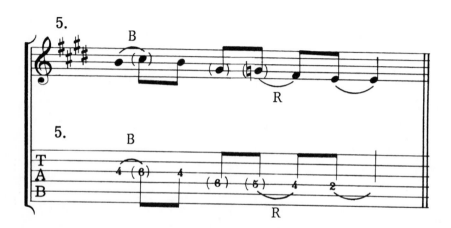

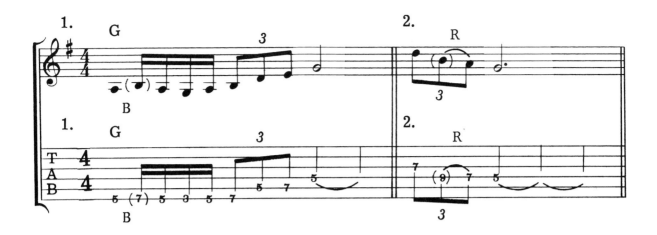

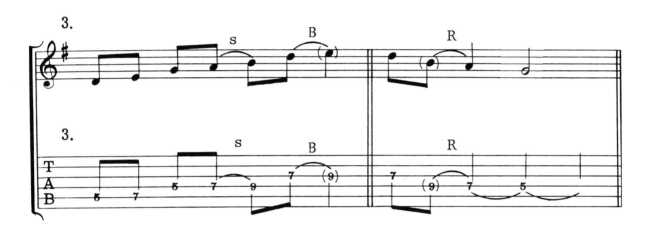

PENTATONIC "SLIDING"

Just as in the blues section, you'll see that the technique of "sliding" between notes can be helpful if you're working in the pentatonic modes. These, again, involve the passing notes and major thirds, and help get you to new positions quickly. For starters, here are the same two positions we've been working with, only now incorporating "slides" into the scales. Licks will start coming to mind just from doing these exercises.

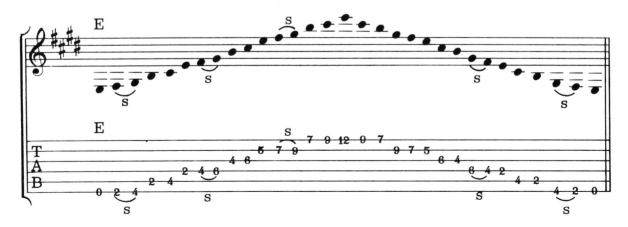

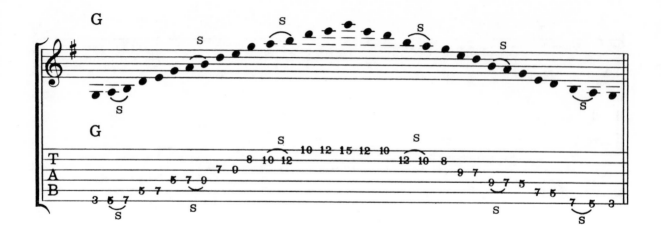

ADDING HAMMER-ONS

Sliding will get you somewhere fast, but combining slides with hammer-ons gets the job done even more efficiently. This scale is a well-crafted blend of not only slides and hammer-ons, but also of barring. Note where the barre enables you to create more hammer-on possibilities. Practice this one until it sounds smooth and you'll always find it to be a good warm-up exercise.

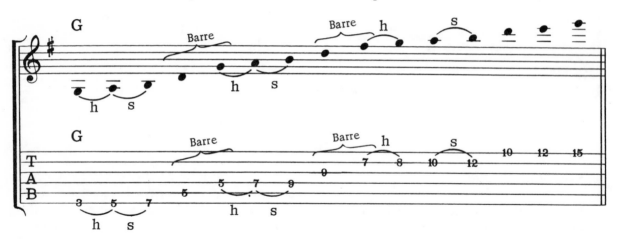

Here is a complicated scale that is an assortment of hammer-ons, slides, *and* pull-offs. This final addition makes it actually possible to play with one hand! Practice it slowly at first, and make sure that the pull-offs are really plucks that give new resonancy to the string. When all seems in order, start speeding it up until you can play it fast and clean.

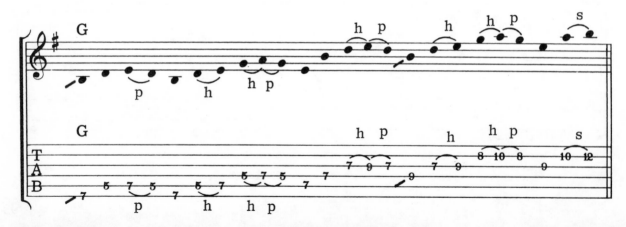

Now that you've seen all the techniques, and how they relate to one another, it would be a good idea to play the licks that follow (as well as try to create some licks on your own that feel unique to you). These are all in the same positions and keys with which we've been working. However, where applicable I've indicated the chords of the key that would best suit the particular lick.

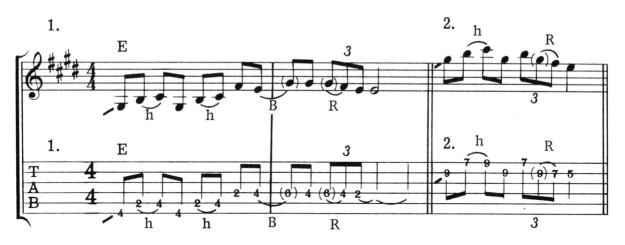

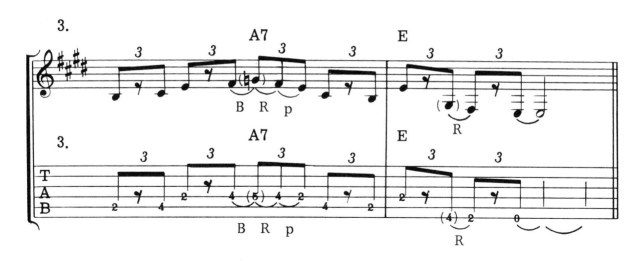

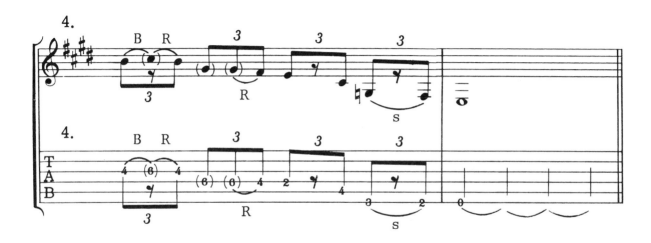

PENTATONIC POSITION NO. 2

This second scale position for the pentatonic mode uses a format that is almost identical to the blues/rock position we worked on earlier in the book. In the following example, this can be illustrated by the new pentatonic position for the key of E. The second group of notes is the blues scale for the same key. Notice how all we've really done is to move the first scale up three frets, or a step and a half.

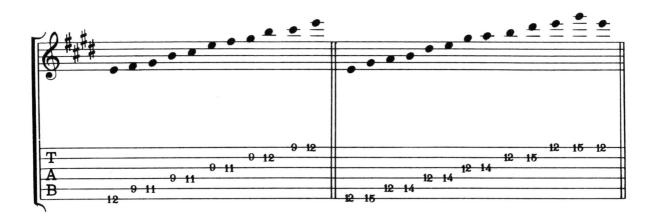

The concept of pentatonic versus blues/rock scales is a useful one to lead guitarists and is a great aid in developing improvisational skills. The main thing to keep in mind is that whatever key you may be playing in, the *major* pentatonic scale will be the minor *blues* scale for the *relative minor chord* of that key. For example, in the case of the key of E, the pentatonic scale becomes the blues scale for C sharp minor. When practicing these scales, try to see how different they sound when juxtaposed against the root or the relative minor chord. For your convenience, Diagram 16 lists all the keys and their relative minor chords:

Root (Tonic)	Relative Minor
A	F#m
A#	Gm
B	G#m
C	Am
C#	A#m
D	Bm
D#	Cm
E	C#m
F	Dm
F#	D#m
G	Em
G#	Fm

Diagram 16

This position of the pentatonic scale lends itself to many possibilities within a relatively small area, giving it a box-like status. It therefore contains many passing-note possibilities and many other notes that can also be added when the situation arises. Here is the scale with the addition of flatted sevenths and minor thirds. See how this creates a much more "bluesy" sound:

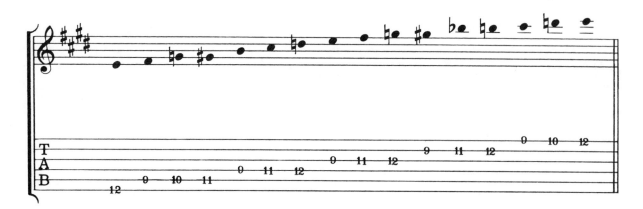

In certain cases, depending on the melodic structure of the music you are playing, you might find it more appropriate to utilize *major* sevenths instead of flatted, as in this example:

LICKS—PENTATONIC POSITION NO. 2

The best way for me to convey the musical ideas that come from using this scale is through the following group of runs. One of the most important and frequently heard uses of passing notes in this scale is that of the flatted third to express the change to the IV chord from the root. This makes sense musically, for when placed against the new IV chord, this minor third now becomes the *seventh*. You'll see this occur many times, and wherever it happens, any chord change that best suits the lick is notated:

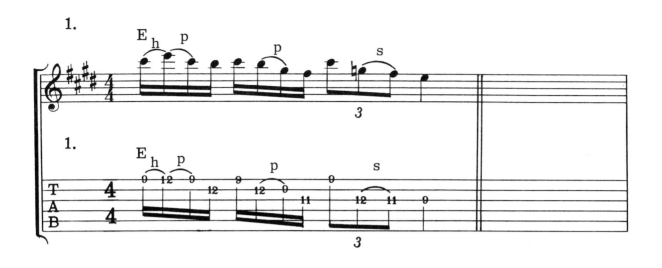

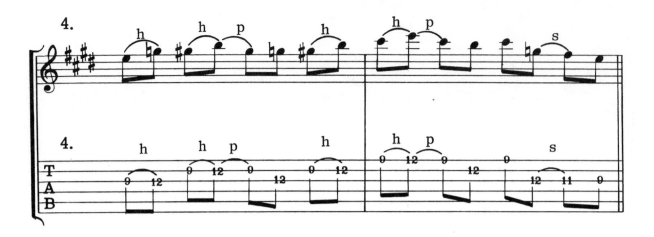

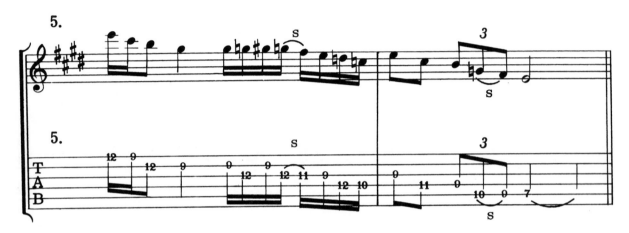

PENTATONIC/BLUES EXERCISE

This is an extended piece designed to illustrate the use of this scale played against its tonic (key) and its relative minor. I'm still using the key of E, and you should be able to recognize some of the licks you just learned in the previous exercise. Even though these scales *are* interchangeable, you should become aware of the subtle differences built into the phrasing and notation that help better define the chord change. In this piece we'll also be involving the first position of the pentatonic scale covered earlier.

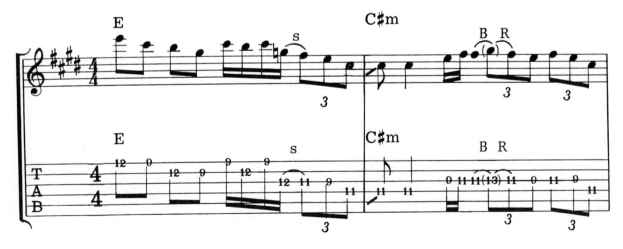

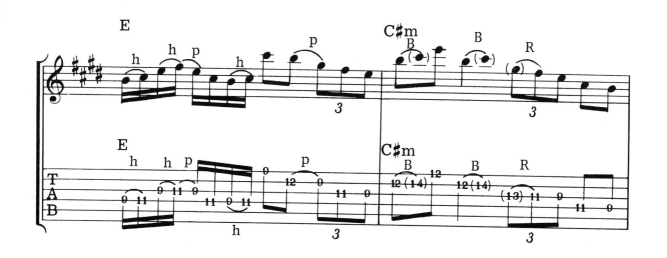

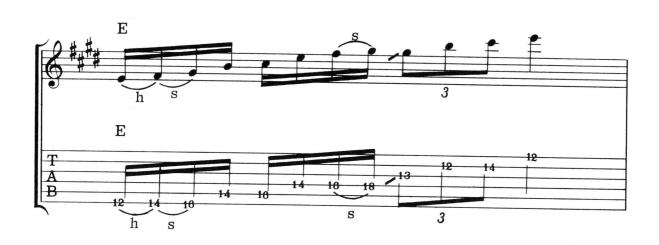

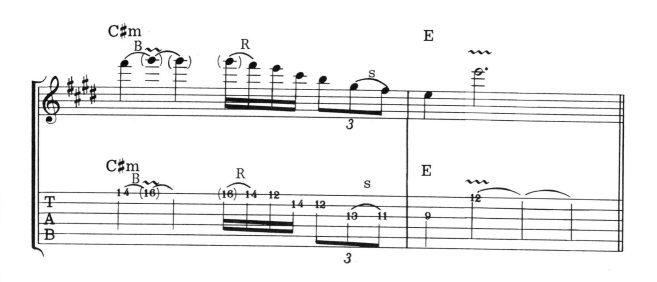

PENTATONIC POSITION NO. 3

In this new position we are essentially "elongating" the position just discussed, and adding to the fluidity that can be achieved with these new, longer positions. Here's the scale, and you should be able to tell just where it crosses over into the last pentatonic box position, and then where it leaves it again.

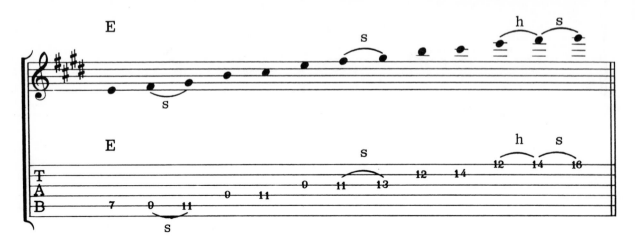

LICKS—PENTATONIC POSITION NO. 3

Here again are a helpful group of ditties that incorporate all the techniques (bending, slid-ing, hammers, pulls, and barring) you've been using. Enjoy them!

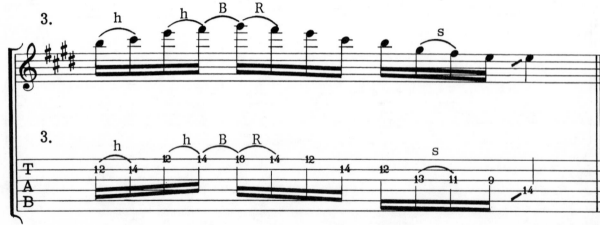

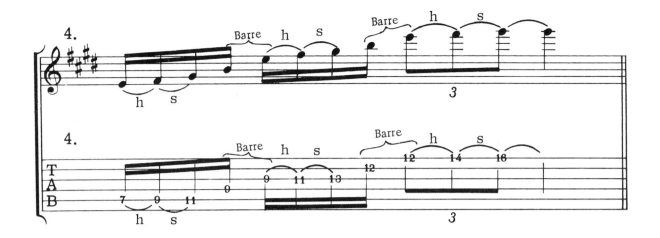

THE B.B. KING PENTATONIC STYLE

One thing is certain; B.B. (Blues Boy) King possesses one of the most recognizable electric-guitar styles around, and is a true master at extracting more emotion from fewer notes than just about anyone. He also was and continues to be a source of great inspiration to me, and was one of my earliest influences. (One might still fall victim to one of my B.B. imitations while seeing me in concert.)

Though a virtuoso of all the blues scales and positions, B.B. King seems to get his greatest mileage out of the pentatonic scale, particularly one box position of it. It is within this one small area that he manages to get a wide variety of expression from the use of string bending, hammers and pulls, and his own unmistakable "butterfly" vibrato. To get a better understanding of what I'm talking about, here is the pentatonic scale with B.B.'s favorite location in brackets:

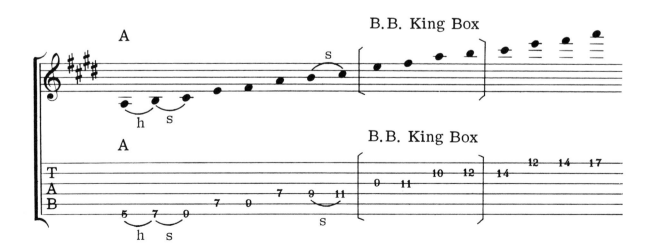

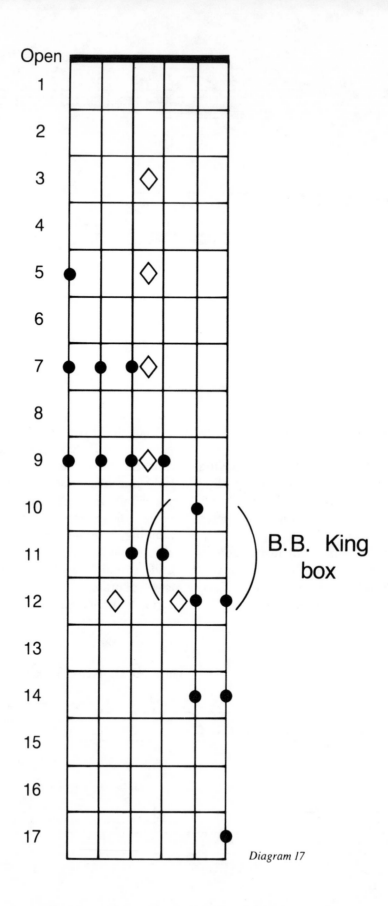

Diagram 17

For a first look into the kinds of things B.B. King and others like to create from this position, here are just a few special licks. You'll see that by bending the B string a *whole step* you go to the major third, and therefore, any lick using this bend is best played against the root, or tonic, chord. In the second example, we're bending the string only a *half step*, thereby making it the minor third, or the flatted *seventh of the IV chord*. This subtle major-third-to-seventh approach is an important part of the blues, and is used often by B.B. King in this position. In the third lick the bend on the twelfth fret of the high E string resolves back to the E after a short excursion up to the F sharp—one of the classic blues licks for the V chord. The fourth lick, another tried and true classic, bends up to the seventh (G natural) and is interchangeable with either the I, IV, or V chord. It would seem, from listening to B.B. King's records, that the bend *must* be a whole step starting on the F note at the thirteenth fret, but many of the older blues men created this lick by making a *step and a half* bend beginning on the E note at the twelfth fret, a note that is still within the box position. Try it both ways, and see which approach is more agreeable to you—you might find the latter approach uncomfortable at first!

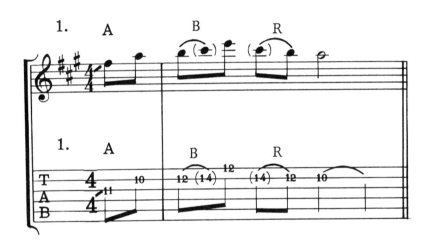

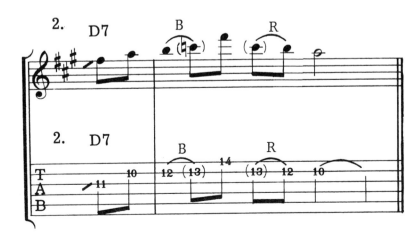

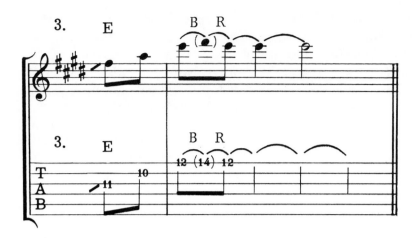

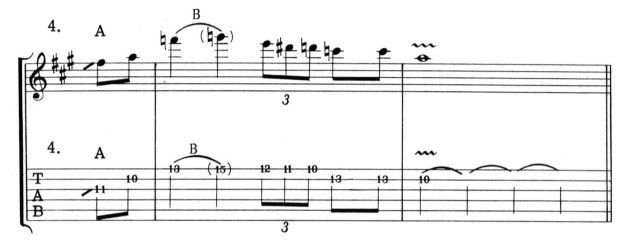

B.B. KING BOX LICKS

Now that you've seen the fundamentals of how many of these licks are arrived at, take a look at the following group of exercises, which consist of the many possibilities that can be found within this particular box position, and a few that venture slightly out of the position. Be sure to notice where the chords are notated, so you can see where the licks best apply.

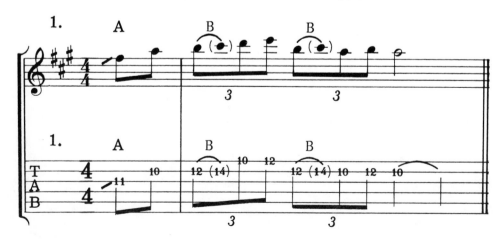

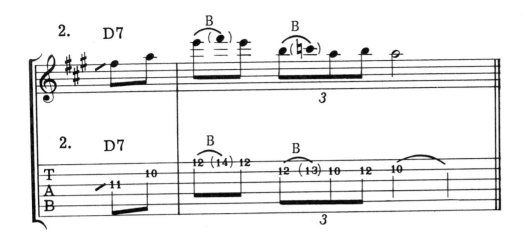

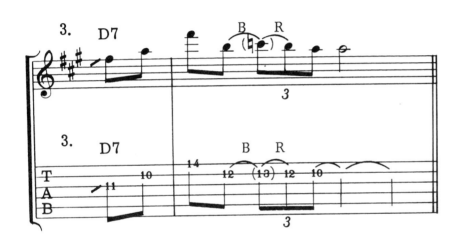

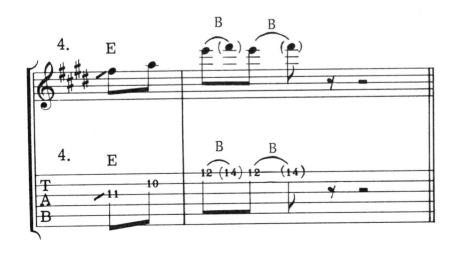

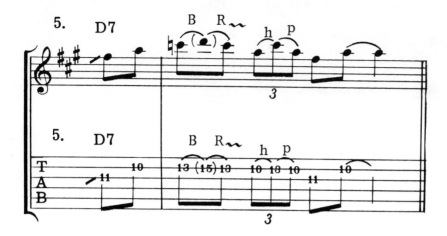

TWELVE-BAR EXERCISE

In this piece, you'll actually be playing an entire twelve-bar solo exercise in the B.B. King blues style. It can be played at any tem-po, but here it is written out with an up-tempo feel in mind. Again, be sure to control your bends and licks to fit the right chords, and be sure to use the "pivoting" so important for the proper vibrato sound.

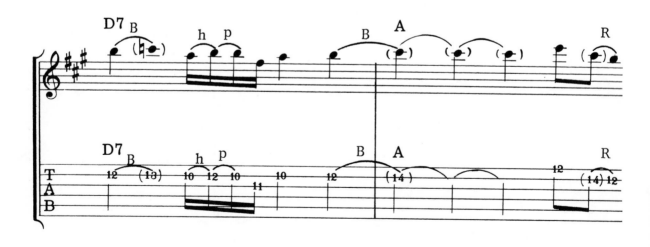

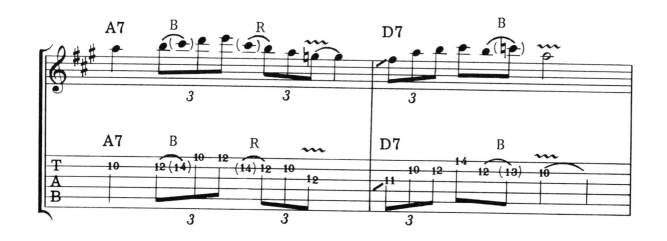

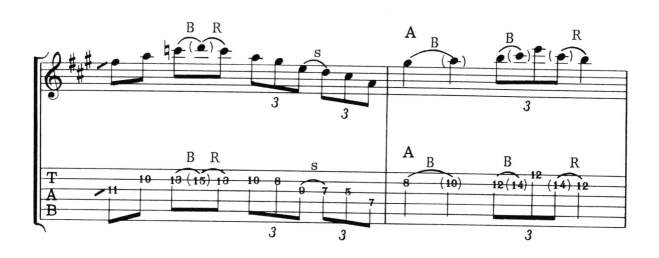

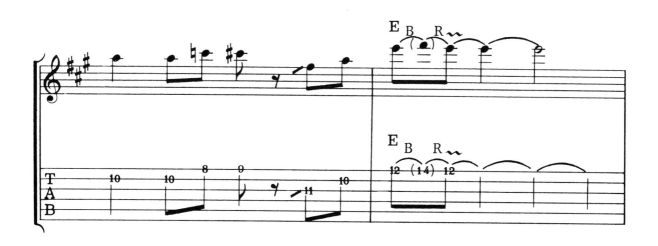

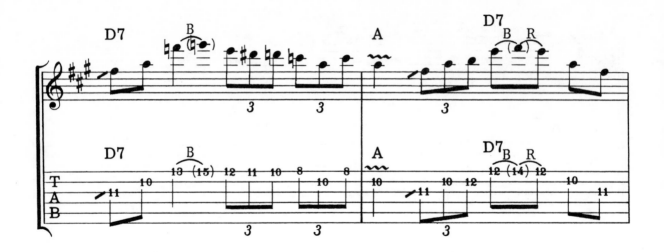

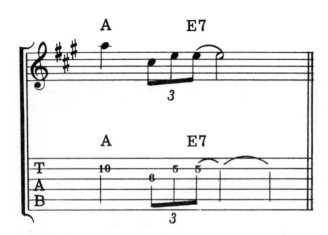

PUTTING IT ALL TOGETHER

This section is a melting pot of lead-guitar techniques, putting together all of the expressive and technical skills we've covered. Slides, pull-offs, hammer-ons, bends, vibrato, barring, and double-stops are all here in the form of full-fledged solos designed to illustrate the many situations the lead electric guitarist can encounter. Try to practice them slowly at first, allowing yourself to speed up as your confidence grows. If there are any particular techniques you feel you should brush up on, refer back. It's the rare guitarist who learns everything in perfect sequence, so don't feel frustrated if you get hung up on a particular technique. We *all* go through it sometimes!

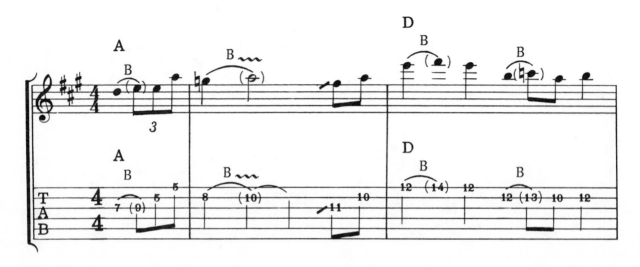

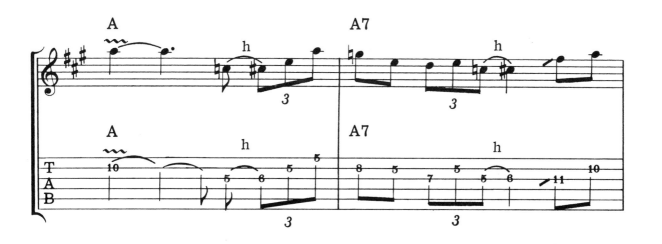

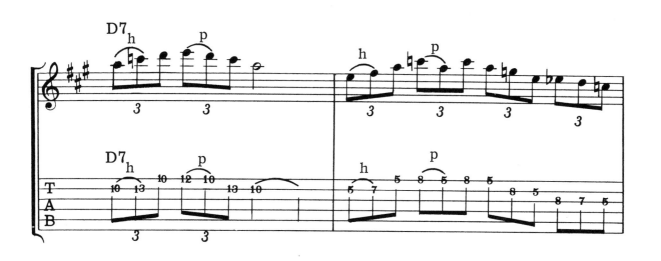

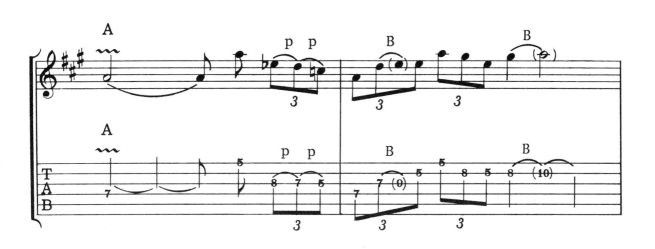

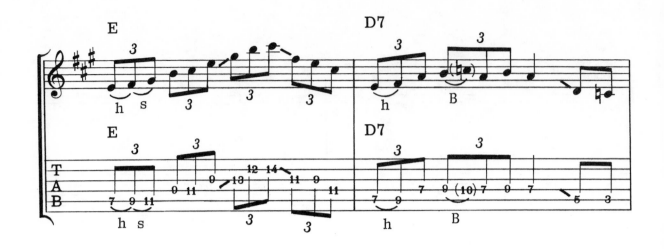

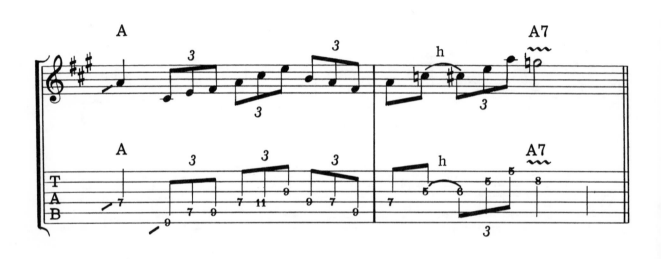

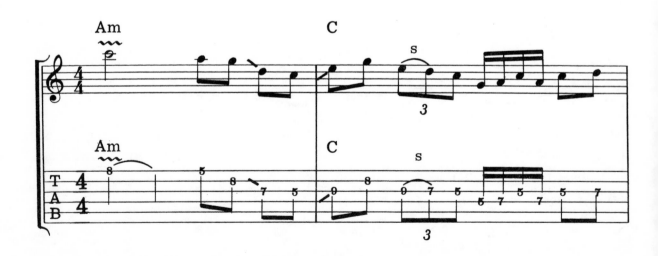

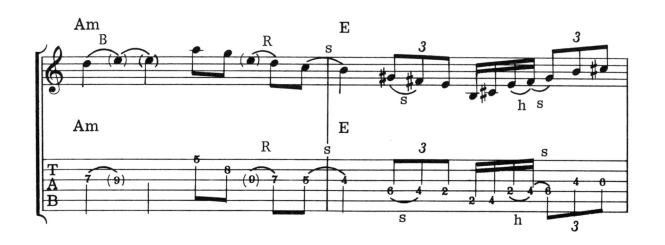

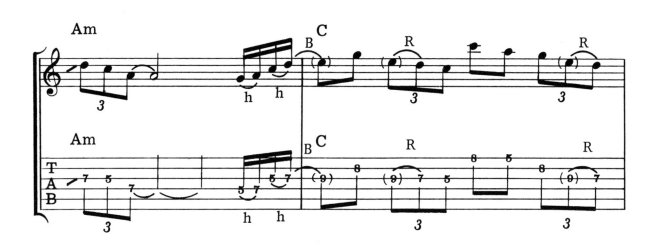

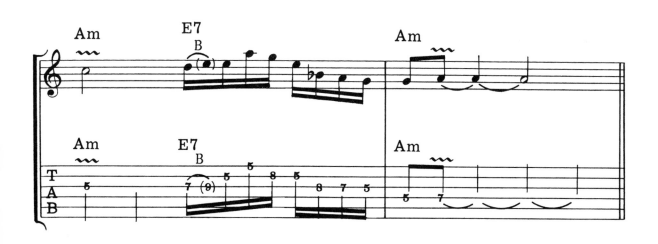

Electric Country Guitar

Country music has been growing and evolving so rapidly over the past fifteen years, that it has influenced almost every other form of music. Rather than dismiss it as elementary, I have made the art of country lead guitar an ongoing learning process that has never failed to bring me renewed joy and artistic satisfaction.

UNIQUE QUALITIES OF COUNTRY LEAD GUITAR

Each style of guitar playing seems to have its own distinct sound. This especially holds true for the country style, and there are several elements involved in this sound. For one, country has generally a "cleaner" sound on the guitar. What this means is that distortion, whether it be from the amp or by more indirect means, is hardly ever used; it is re-placed by crisp, clear notes (this points to certain preferred guitar-and-amp setups discussed later in the book). Harmonized licks are more common, using two, sometimes three notes played simultaneously. String bending, while important in almost any style of guitar playing, holds a special place in the country player's heart. Almost all country music uses guitars played with metal or glass slides, such as pedal steels, Hawaiian guitars, and Dobros. All this tends to influence the sound of country lead guitar, making bending an indispensable tool for the country lead player.

THE BASIC COUNTRY PROGRESSION

For reference and familiarity, we'll be using this progression through most of this chapter. It represents many of the most often heard country songs, and works well in many tempos. Here it is for the key of G:

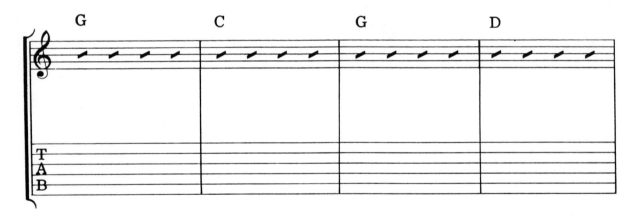

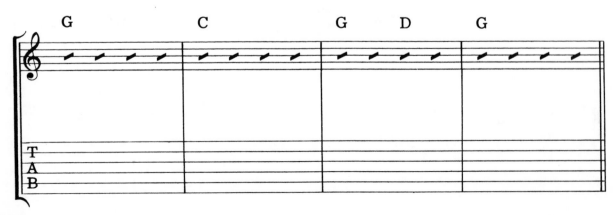

THE BLUEGRASS LICK

This country lick is most often heard as a fill or ending lick played by the guitarist in bluegrass music, an acoustic wing of country music that has its origins in the music of Bill Monroe and the state of Kentucky. Here it is for both G and C; you can try flat-picking each note, or using the indicated hammer-ons and pull-offs for a more fluid sound:

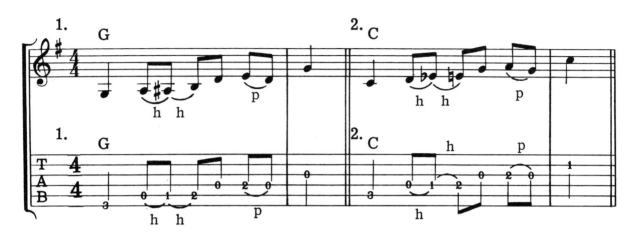

This solo exercise based on the country progression in G utilizes the bluegrass lick for the G, C, and D chords. Practice it slowly at first, then work up to being able to create a clean sound at a fast tempo:

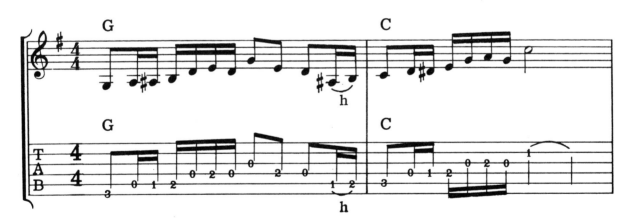

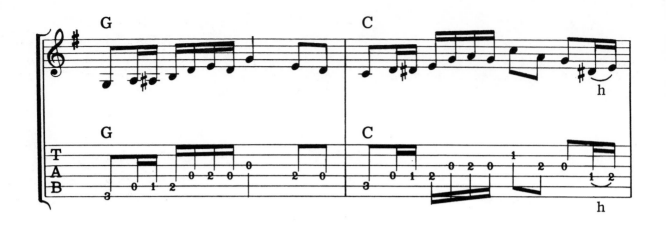

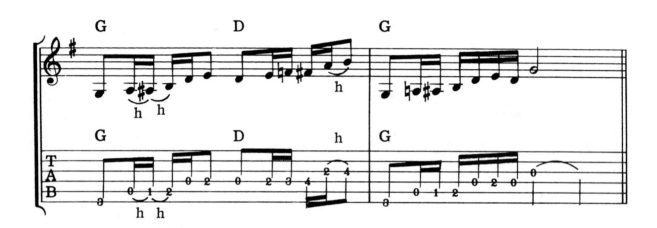

PENTATONIC COUNTRY LICKS

The pentatonic scale, with which you are already familiar, is the most commonly used scale in all forms of country lead guitar. The same slides, passing notes, and general techniques are used in country, but it is the *phrasing* of the licks that sets them apart. Here, for example, is a collection of some of my favorite country licks for the open G pentatonic position:

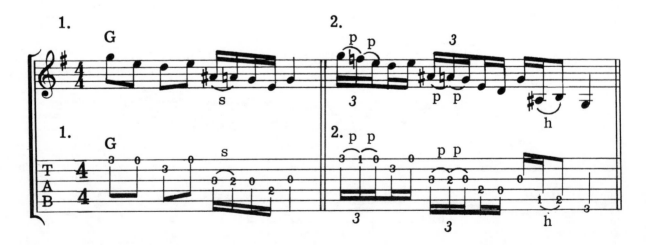

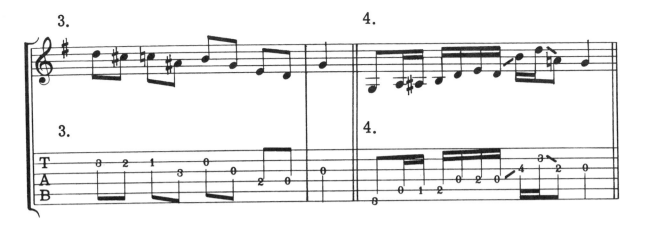

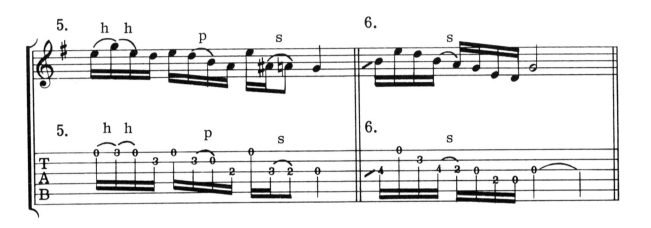

If we take this position up higher, to a *closed* location such as in A, you can see the many new possibilities, as well as some of the obvious limitations, that result from losing all those nice, juicy open strings!

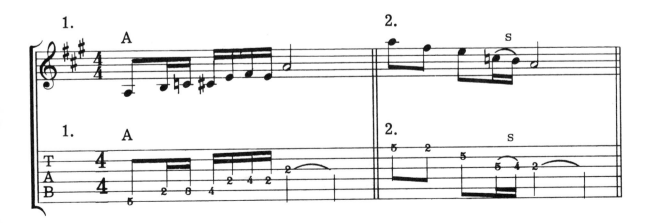

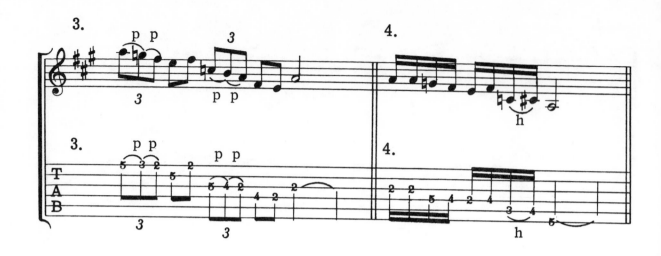

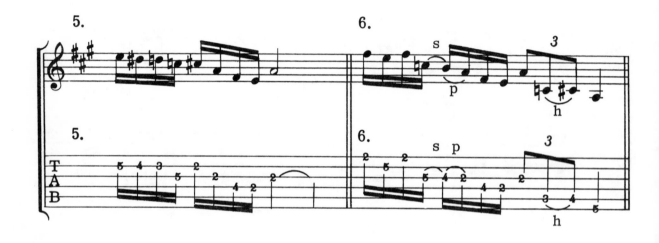

Getting back to G, we see here the wide range of country lick possibilities in the longer, *closed* pentatonic position no. 2:

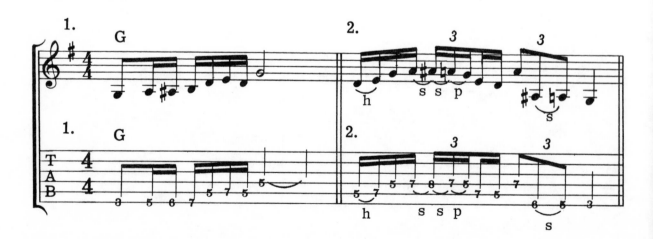

COUNTRY HAMMER-ONS

When I first started listening to country pickers, in the mid-sixties, string bending had not evolved much beyond the good old one-string "slur." Hammer-ons, though, were common, and the use of other notes in harmony with the hammered note was quite obvious in the playing of Zal Yanovsky, lead guitarist with the Lovin' Spoonful. This style is quite a bit like country piano playing, especially that of the great Floyd Cramer.

There are open and closed positions for these hammer-ons, and some resolve to the chord, while others require an additional pull-off for resolution. Here are the open-position hammer-ons for the open G, C, A, and D chords:

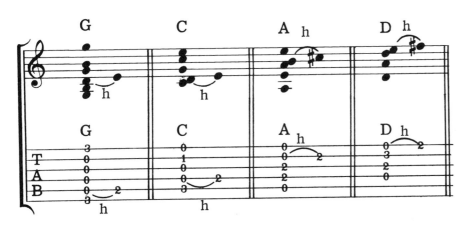

Here are the important closed positions. Note where the licks are simple in their execution, and where some require more complex arrangements to finally resolve:

HAMMER-ON SOLO

Here is a full-fledged solo using these hammer-on positions for the country progression we've been working with. Try to be aware of the particular chord positions you'll be resolving to in this piece:

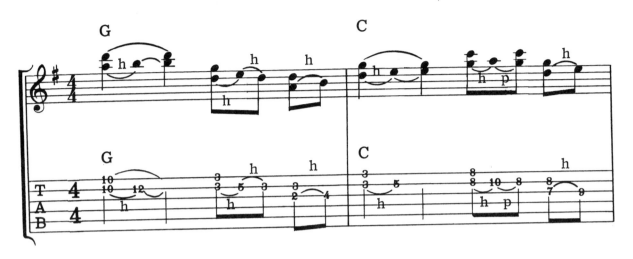

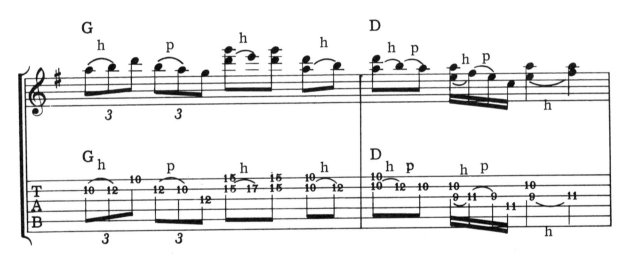

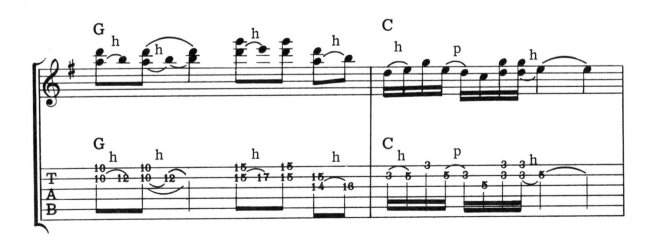

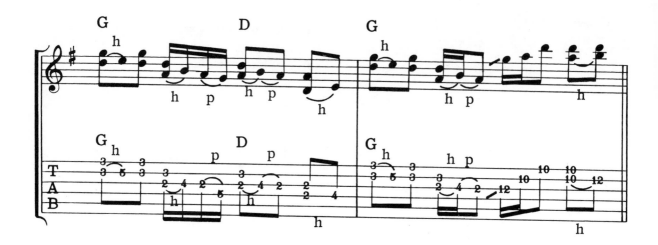

LEARNING TO USE THE PICK AND FINGERS TOGETHER

This is a technique rarely talked about, yet widely used and versatile. This is the proper time to introduce you to it, because it might make the material that follows (and guitar playing in general) more productive for you.

Years ago, when faced with the desire to play double-note licks, particularly the kind that are separated by one or more strings, I found that combining flat and finger-picked techniques was the best route to take. Two great advantages of this style are, first, you no longer need to be involved with the tricky right-hand damping, and second, you can always go back to using just the flat pick for rhythm work. This use of pick and fingers also enables you to play some complicated "roll" patterns that we'll be discussing later. You'll also find the advantage of being able to "grab" the notes simultaneously a great improvement over the less synchronized use of flat pick and damping to create double-stops.

SINGLE-NOTE PLAYING

Keep in mind that this is essentially a three-note technique and, when playing single-note lead, requires the use of lower strings than the top three. The unit of pick, middle finger, and ring finger should now embrace the three strings that include the *new* string. Here is a photo of the "ready to play" position for using the top three strings in this style:

Therefore, in playing this "backtrack" scale, be consciously moving the pick and fingers toward the low E string as the run introduces new strings:

In this brief piece you get a chance to use this new picking style to play the G and high E strings, leaving out the B string, in between. After plucking each note, try to return the pick or finger to the "ready" position; this will also act as an involuntary damping technique after a while. You should also try some double-note runs on the D and B strings using the same picking technique.

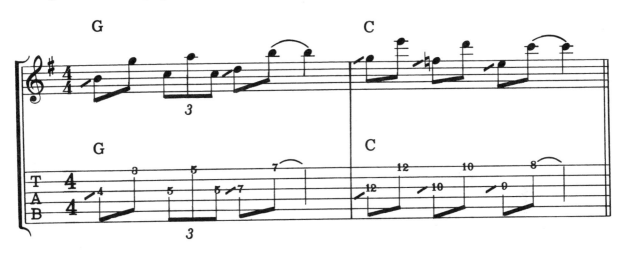

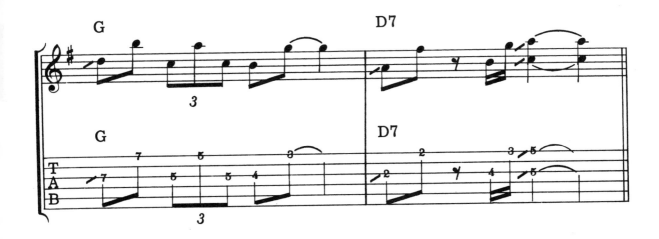

COUNTRY "ROLL" PATTERNS

The idea of creating almost banjo-like "roll" patterns is one of the more exciting uses of this pick/finger technique I have found, and it helps to create a bright, clean country sound while developing greater independence of the right hand.

In this exercise, a rather complex one, see how we change the patterns back and forth, while always maintaining the two drone strings on top. We're creating what seems to be a fairly wide spread of the fingers with some parts of this exercise, so beware—it might not come easy to you at first. It also helps to imagine the sound of a bright, sustaining banjo, to play these rolls in their proper spirit:

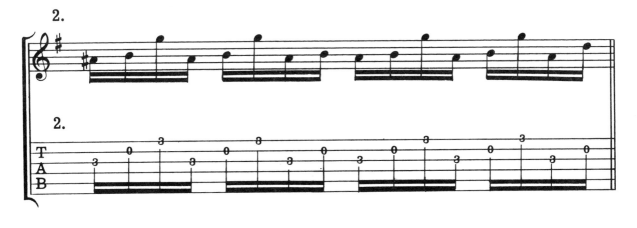

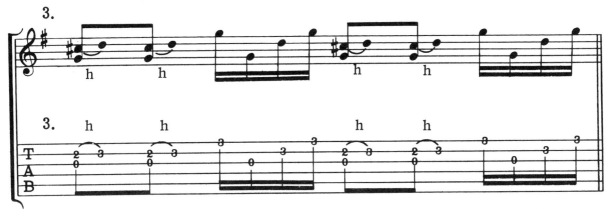

COUNTRY STRING-BENDING TECHNIQUES

One of my favorite subjects as well as one of the more demanding techniques around, it makes sense to follow the section on how to play with your pick and fingers combined, because this technique is well put to use in country string bending.

When I first started to develop this technique, I was taken with the sound of the pedal steel players in country music. The sound of strings sustaining while others were bending was something I just *had* to have, and I even *did* take up the pedal steel for a while. It was translating this elusive sound to the guitar that held my fancy, though, and it still does. Clarence White, the late, great lead guitarist with the Byrds, had in the late sixties, along with Gene Parsons, invented a B-string bender that pulled the B string of the guitar up a whole step—very much like the principle of the pedal steel guitar. With this device it's possible to turn an Asus.2 position containing an open B string to a fully resolved A major chord. I was deeply influenced by Clarence's playing with the Byrds, and as a result, created a style that was totally mine because I had no idea the B-string bender even existed until years after I started to copy the sound I heard on those records! I've been exploring this style for quite some time now, and I'm sure you'll find yourself getting hooked on it as I did in my developing days.

There are two major qualities that country string bending has that set it apart from the other styles we've been discussing. First, it is much "cleaner" and more precise in its execution than, say, blues bending, which has a more emotional approach and more built-in possibilities than clean country bending. The other quality found in country bends is that they are often played with other notes in harmony. This is the "pedal steel" effect; we'll be discussing the technique in this chapter.

COUNTRY STRING BENDING AS SUBSTITUTION

Just as we found in the blues/rock section, it's often helpful to think of bend licks initially as *substitutions* for licks that were played with other techniques. In the case of country lead guitar, the techniques most often displaced are hammer-ons and pull-offs. In this example, you can see how a major-third hammer-on for the A position of C now becomes a whole-step bend that has a note in harmony with it:

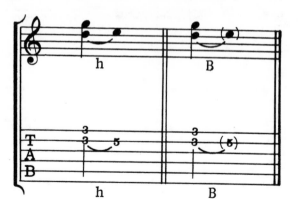

In this lick, a country "ending" lick can be created by using a combination of the same bend, only in different positions. Here the chords move F, C, G, C. You can see that we are going back and forth between the A positions (bent) and the E positions (unbent) of each of the chords.

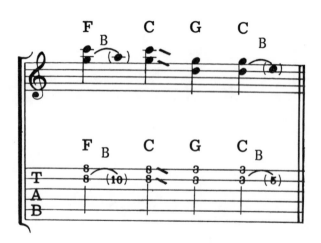

In this bend involving the G string, you can create an easier situation than the hammer-on for which you're actually substituting. I've also written it here with a high-E-string harmony; try to utilize the pick-and-finger technique for this. Remember to keep using the other fingers behind the bend to help it along. This will aid in getting that mechanical "pedal steel" effect.

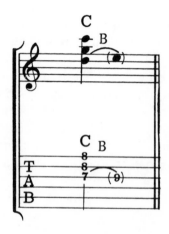

Combine the two bend positions in this position, and you'll see the melodic as well as chordal potential of string bending within closed box positions. Here is a substitution first for a hammer-pull lick, then a hammer:

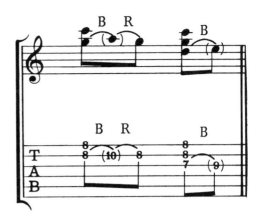

Suspended-fourth licks are also popular in country lead playing; they imitate an often heard sound in pedal-steel playing. Here are examples of both E-position and A-position suspended fourths. Take note that these are examples of *half-step* bends, as opposed to whole-steps, and that you should *have the bend prepared to be released at the start of the lick.* This might take some time before it feels right to you, but after a while you become quite used to the way a particular bend should feel.

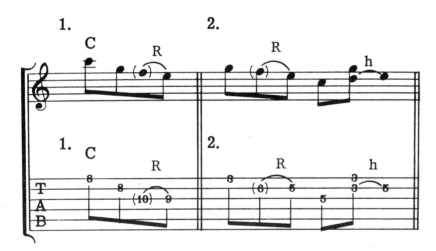

In the case of three-note licks such as these "pedal steel" bends, use the pick, middle finger and ring finger together. This will give you the flexibility to play them all at once or to create more inventive single-note lines within the position.

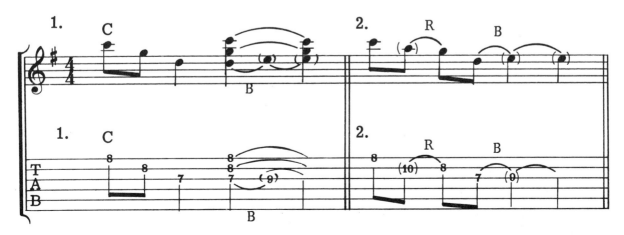

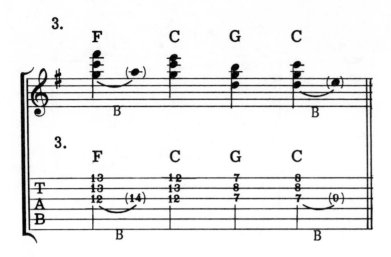

3.

BENDS COMBINED WITH SEVENTHS

Sevenths are useful in creating a feeling of change or anticipation within a lick, and hold many possibilities for the creative mind. In the first seventh position, we are taking the last major triad we just worked on and dropping the root note a whole step to the seventh. Be careful, because the index finger, which was helping the bend along, must now play the seventh, leaving the second finger all alone to bend for itself.

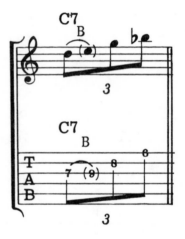

This position is unusual, because the initial position is already a seventh, and the bend becomes merely a melodic grace note that floats over the chord and then returns back to its original position. This lick is also useful just before the chord is about to change. In this case, the most likely chord we would be going to is F, the IV chord.

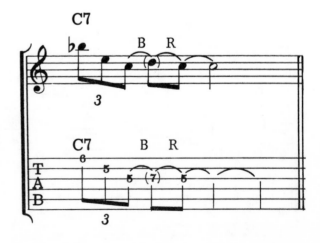

"PEDAL STEEL" LICKS

The next group of runs explores the many possibilities available within this string-bending style on the top three strings. Some illustrate the combination of non-bend with bend licks, enabling you to experiment with the more impromptu aspects of string bending in the country style.

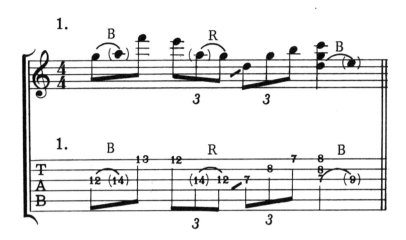

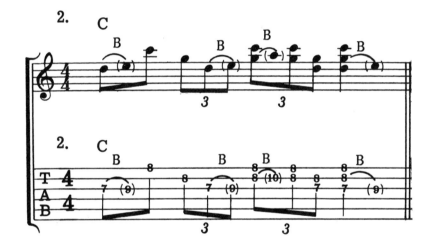

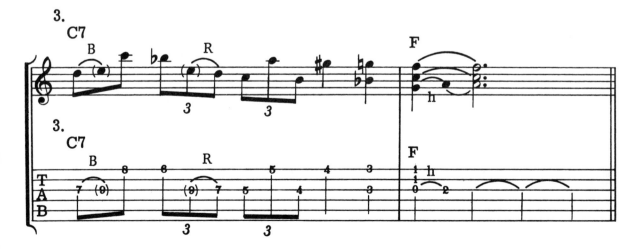

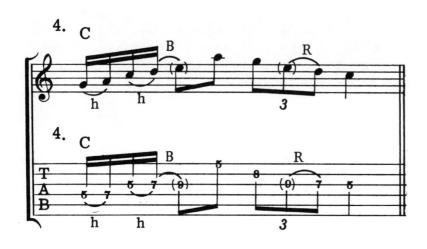

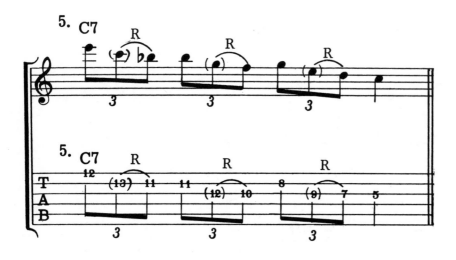

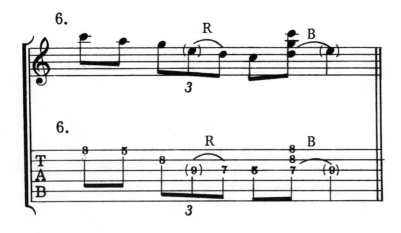

COUNTRY STRING-BENDING SOLO

In this solo piece, I've taken a standard country progression and used string bending to its fullest. You'll see just where the sevenths fit in and how helpful the pick/finger-pick approach is to this style of playing. Hope you enjoy it!

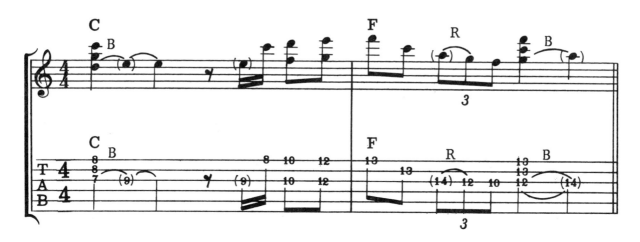

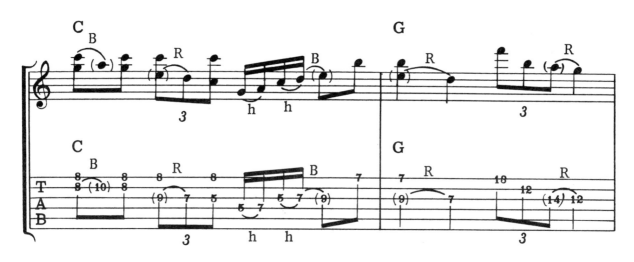

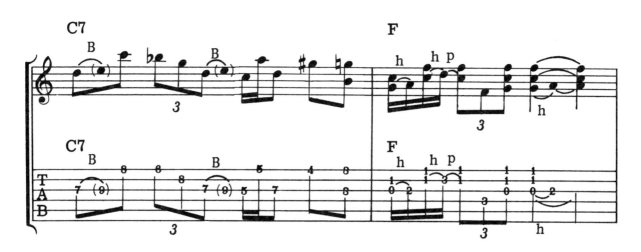

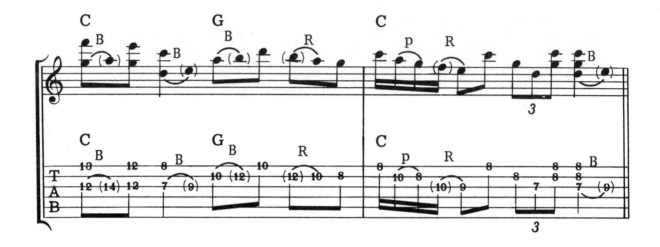

ROCKABILLY RHYTHMS

Rockabilly was one of the earliest forms of rock 'n' roll, and as its name implies, was actually a hybrid of hillbilly (or country) styles and rock 'n' roll rhythms. The main exponents of this style were Elvis Presley (with Scotty Moore on guitar), Carl Perkins (the creator of "Blue Suede Shoes," "Matchbox," "Honey Don't," and many other hits), Eddie Cochran ("Summertime Blues"), Gene Vincent and the Bluecaps ("Be-Bop-A-Lula," with Cliff Gallup on guitar), and Buddy Holly and the Crickets.

These bands were often quite small, and this made the guitarists, out of necessity, play involved parts that included at times rhythm, lead, and bass work combined. Heel damping was often used, and an almost "Travis-picked" independence of notes was often heard in the playing of the more advanced rockabilly players such as Cliff Gallup and Carl Perkins, who were obviously influenced by the wonderful fingerpicking of Merle Travis, the developer of this style.

There are three rhythm licks heard most often in early rockabilly, and they each have a sound that brings to mind classic recordings. This rhythm lick, for instance, is reminiscent of the playing by Scotty Moore on the very early Elvis recordings of "Mystery Train," "That's All Right," and "My Baby Left Me." Note how the slide up to the A7 chord position helps set a better mood for this lick.

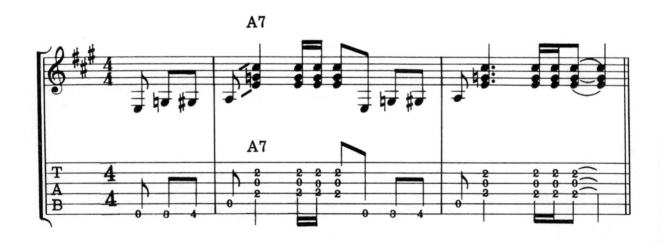

I call this rhythm pattern the "gospel lick," because it so closely resembles the accompaniment often heard in traditional gospel music. It works best for the A7 position, enabling your left hand to be freer while the open A string can be used as a bass note. Keep in mind that the first finger barre covers only the B, G, and D strings and should serve to cut out or damp the high E string.

In this final rockabilly pattern for the key of E, we are recalling the great playing of Carl Perkins, one of rock 'n' roll's founding fathers and a tremendous influence on the Beatles and countless other musicians of the past two and a half decades. This rhythm lick contains a melodic structure similar to what is found in more complex finger-picked parts, and is heard on songs like "Honey Don't," "Everybody's Tryin' to Be My Baby," and "Blue Suede Shoes." Keep a close lookout for those hammer-ons!

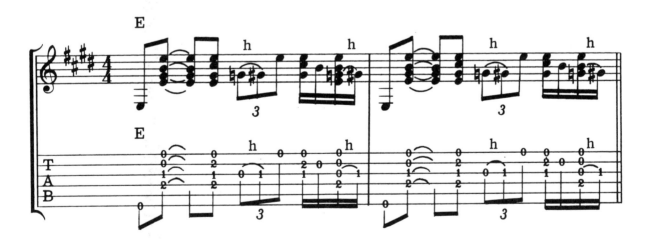

4

Equipment—What to Use and When

The discussion of musical equipment, or "talking shop," is to some an obsession, to others a bore. To all of us, however, it's still a necessity, and when I set out to write this book, I realized that no overview of electric guitar would be complete without it.

Electric music has come a long way, and like everything else, its rate of evolution has been increasing at an astounding rate. The equipment found in an average bar band today must be at least three times what was required in the early days of rock 'n' roll, and must cost at least ten times as much! Music can still be created under minimal conditions, but there is now a tremendous variety of guitars, amps, and effects available to the average player, and it's important that your money be spent wisely.

What Guitar Is Best for You?

This is, of course, the most important piece of equipment you'll own and has a great deal to do with your style and the kind of sound you want to put across. Many professionals and amateurs have several guitars for their various needs. (I am no exception, with a collection numbering close to fifty. All actually have specific uses in my own music, and any other performance or recording dates I might get called on to play.)

THE HOLLOW-BODY ELECTRIC

This is the earliest form of electric guitar, and is still used by jazz players of the older school, such as Tal Farlow, Joe Pass, and George Benson. It had its place in rock 'n' roll, too, with early players like Chuck Berry, Scotty Moore, and Bill Haley. For today's music, however, it would be hard to recommend this guitar if you expect to be heard over a band. This is because nonsolid guitars tend to feed back at high volumes (the body resonates too much), and it is for this reason I would recommend them only for quieter, more intimate situations such as jazz with a small combo.

THE SEMIHOLLOW ELECTRIC GUITAR

In the mid-fifties the changes that were taking place in music required the creation of something in between a solid-body guitar (which was still considered too radical by the guitar establishment) and the tried and true but too cumbersome hollow-body. The double cutaway semihollow guitar was the answer, and Gibson created a line that included the ES 335, 345, and 355, all semihollow instruments. These guitars had f-holes, like the traditional hollow-bodies, but were thinner and were filled in the middle between the f-holes to help eliminate feedback.

One of the best ways to decide on what guitar you'd like to play is by listening to the various types played by well-known artists. For example, when you hear someone like Larry Carlton, he's almost always playing an ES 335, a guitar that has become his trademark. When you're listening to B.B. King playing "Lucille," you're really hearing a Gibson ES 355, the top of the line of the ES series. Here is an example of an early, very rare "blond" ES 335.

Semihollow electric guitar

SOLID-BODY ELECTRICS

This, of course, is the most widely accepted form of the electric guitar because of its comfort, feedback elimination, playability, and flexibility of design. Thanks to pioneering geniuses like Les Paul, Leo Fender, and Paul Bigsby, the electric guitar has become an instrument that can meet all challenges. Oddly, with all the changes that solid-body guitars go through year after year, the three originals, the Gibson Les Paul and the Fender Telecaster and Stratocaster, all remain the most popular and classically designed. This is testimony to the foresight and brilliance of these early guitar makers who were to change music forever.

Here are early examples of each of these classics, now highly prized by players and collectors alike.

1952 Gold-top Les Paul

1953 Fender Telecaster

1958 Fender Stratocaster

THE FENDER SOUND VERSUS THE GIBSON SOUND

Two distinct schools of thought can be categorized this way. While there are many more manufacturers today than Gibson and Fender, most continue to mimic these two great pioneers.

The difference I see in these types of instruments and what they inspire in the guitarist can best be traced through my own experiences with discovering them, and how they changed my approach to playing.

Certain guitars can make you do certain things, especially at the times in your life when a musical change is in the stars. I know that if it were not for the right guitar coming along at the right time, certain aspects of my playing might not have evolved in just the way they did. For example, during high school, where there was a big blues boom going on, old Les Pauls were said to be great blues guitars. I had never played one, and wasn't even sure what one really looked like. I had been playing a Guild hollow-body electric, but I felt it was time for a change. So I put on order an expensive, classy-looking hollow-body made by another leading guitar maker. When it finally arrived, not only was it in the wrong finish, but with the very first note I bent, the nut completely broke off, sending strings flying in all directions and the salesman off to refund my money. Feeling disappointed, I suspected that perhaps the quality of the new guitars was starting to decline. Well, I went around the corner to an obscure shop where I fell in love with and bought a 1952 gold-top Les Paul. By the way, it was considerably cheaper than the bomb I had just played around the corner.

That guitar had a profound effect on me. Its ease of playability and incredible sustaining qualities opened up new musical doors. With that Les Paul, I spent five years performing, practicing, and developing my overall expressiveness on the guitar, and found it to be well suited for blues and slide playing, especially at higher volumes. This is generally true of the Gibson-style instruments (most people prefer to play them loud). I'm not saying that a particularly fine solid-body Gibson won't sound great at low volumes too, but many jazz musicians prefer using a semihollow- or all-hollow-body guitar.

After four years of making the rounds with that gold-top Les Paul, I moved to Woodstock, New York, and started to back up some of the acts who were living and playing there. The band I was a member of required from me a more subtle approach plus a greater range of tonal variation. Fenders were starting to catch my eyes and ears even though they really had not yet come into vogue on the East Coast. I had my heart set on finding a vintage *Stratocaster,* with no luck for some time, when out of the blue, a friend drove by with a 1954 "Strat" in his trunk that someone else was trying to sell for $75! (I knew this piece was old, but I didn't know till much later that 1954 was the year Fender *introduced* the *Stratocaster!*) To make a pleasant story short, I got my hands on that guitar and was off and running into an entirely new approach. The Fender sound added clarity and subtlety to my tone and attack. Its added bite and sustain at low volumes enabled me to fully explore country techniques and string bending.

The most recent change took place in 1975, when I got the guitar with which I'm now most associated, my 1953 Fender *Telecaster.* This was the first solid-body electric guitar ever mass-marketed (originally called the *Broadcaster* in 1948–49) and still remains one of the most tried and true no-frills guitars around. The early models have *unbelievable* sustain, especially on the treble pickup, and this instrument even further enhanced my string-bending style and my use of harmonic overtones. Other well-known *Tele* players include Roy Buchanan, Roy Nichols, James Burton, and Albert Lee. The biting, singing tone of the *Tele* is truly in a class by itself.

CHOOSING THE GUITAR FOR YOU

As you can see, my style evolved from the combination of various desires to create and what was around to create *on.* I now use all of these guitars for various situations, and each has its own specific application and vocabulary of sounds.

If you're just starting out, it might be worth it to check out the type of guitar that is played by your favorite player. For example, if you love Ted Nugent, you might want to play a Gibson Byrdland. You might be surprised, though, to find this guitar totally unsuited to your own hands, while another instrument

might captivate you on the spot. Don't forget how I ended up with my Les Paul! Go to a store where the salespeople aren't too pushy, and ask to try out and compare various types of guitars. Remember to play through an amp that won't disguise the sound too much, and to accurately record your impressions. I would then recommend sleeping on it (unless the guitar of your dreams might be gone the next day). If there is one that really seems to keep you awake, go back the next day and see if your feelings still hold. The search might still be a much longer one, but don't give up till your hands, heart, and pocketbook are satisfied!

VINTAGE VERSUS NEW

Being an avid guitar collector since the mid-sixties, I'd probably be expected to sound the horn for vintage electrics only, shunning those sleek, new beauties that call out to you from the window of your local music store. Well, take heart. Though this might have once been the case, especially during the transitional period of the mid-sixties, when all guitars seemed to be going down an endless hill, it is only half the story now. Sure, I cherish my '53 Telecaster and my '58 Strat, and I find the certain *quality* that a vintage guitar has in my hands to be something beyond description, a bit like a dream you can't quite remember but you know you enjoyed. There is one simple yet crucial point to remember: these guitars were all once new! Not exactly a revelation, but the point is that the quality acquired by age is only part of the picture with old guitars. What truly makes them great is the way they were *made.*

Back in the mid-fifties, when Les Pauls, Teles, and Strats were being made, there was only a modest demand for them, which made it possible to limit the "assembly line" aspects of manufacture while still retaining a high level of care and workmanship. Just after the Beatles boom, in the mid-sixties, the major companies began to lose sight of what originally made them great, when they lowered quality in an effort to meet the tremendously increased demand for electric guitars. This went on for years, and alienated many a new guitar buyer. It will take something of equally grand proportions to bring our respect back. There is, however, one happy result. This so-called "down" period in American guitar manufacture, along with an increase in popularity for the vintage instruments, has helped to spawn a new, independent breed of luthiers. These guitar makers brought a long-lost dedication back to their craft, and have been winning over professionals and amateurs alike with their blend of old and new refinements.

Pictured below is a guitar made by a contemporary master, Mark Simon, who incorporates the best of both worlds—solid body and arch top—in the making of his guitars.

Phil Kubicki, a master West Coast luthier, has been doing magnificent things as well, and his new "mini" series, featuring the Express and the Arrow, are forerunners in miniature guitar design. Truly destined to become classics!

Pickups

This is a crucial subject because it's the pickup that, after all, is largely responsible for the sound of the electric guitar. Pickups can be broken down into two main categories: single-coil and double-coil. Both of these types have equally unique and valid sounds, and appeal to different types of player. The Fender-type sound has always been associated with the single-coil pickup, creating a crystal-clear, bright tone with plenty of highs in it, while the "humbucker," or double-coil pickup, created for Gibson in the late 1950s, is more linked with the fat, round tone of the Gibson guitars. Gibson also made a great single-coil pickup, called the P-90. This is their older-style pickup (pictured on page 134 on my '52 Les Paul) and while it has the hum problems associated with most single-coil pickups, its lovely, round sound is well worth all the buzzing!

There is also a great deal of controversy surrounding vintage versus new pickups, with the snob appeal of the "Patent Applied For" humbuckers, and the early flat-pole-piece Tele pickups leading the way. One thing is sure: the old pickups *do* sound better. The real question is *why*. These days, it seems there is only one man who *truly* knows, and the answer is in his pickups. His name is Seymour Duncan, and he has built an entire empire on the fact that the old pickups do sound better, and that he can re-create those great sounds. He's also changing the shape of guitar history with other advances such as his "stacked" humbucking pickups and his special "hot-wired" pickups. The following is an assortment of Seymour Duncan pickups, featuring a large variety, including both single- and double-coil types.

Choosing an Amplifier

This is a tricky subject, because tastes vary so, but one thing can be stated unequivocally: tube amps sound better than transistors! This is widely known; yet many guitarists continue to blindly use transistor amps, choking off all the natural sound qualities of their guitars. Some excellent new amps are being made that are hybrids of both tube and transistor designs, and I'm also happy to see that many are finally being made small again, for which we are all thankful!

I've always been partial to the early Fender amps, in fact to *most* pre-1965 amps. They seem to respond more naturally to the touch with less coloration of sound. This is mainly due to the tubes, which "know" *just* when to overload to give that perfect amount of distortion, and the speakers, which seem to "know" the same set of rules. To my ear, the problems start when the speakers are too "clean" for the power rating of the amp, or when the power rating is too high for the particular speaker. The best thing to do is to try several out, so you get a good feel for what your sound should be before you make any hasty decisions. You should also, of course, avoid getting something too small or large for the situations in which you'll be playing (or for the car you'll be loading up!). Try to find the amp that fills as many of your requirements as possible. It's out there; don't worry.

An assortment of vintage Fender amplifiers

Effects Boxes

No discussion of the electric guitar would be complete without mentioning effects boxes. There are a growing number on the market now—phasers, flangers, choruses, delays, distortion boxes, and octave dividers, to name a few—and they are being used more and more, both live and recorded.

The studio guitarist is someone who cannot afford to *not* have all the effects. This is because you'll never know what sound the producer may suddenly want out of you, and as a studio specialist, you're *expected* to have the full bag of tricks.

I've always been something of a purist, and I enjoy getting as much out of the guitar as possible *without* all of these gadgets. Still, they go in and out of vogue like any new fashion, and they're fun to try. Just remember, don't bury your sound in effects to the point of not knowing *what* you're going for. Effects boxes are great tools in the hands of someone with creative restraint and vision, yet they are also deadly aural weapons in the hands of the unenlightened! Be careful.

In Conclusion

It's always difficult to conclude that which is a beginning part of an ongoing process. What I know is merely what was set down before me, added to my own particular approach, and now is once again passed on through this book. What you, the student or teacher, does with it from here can *only* be your own, for we all possess our own personal approach to creating sound, sort of our own "fingerprint," as I like to call it. It's for this important reason that we must be careful to never lose sight of our own approach toward guitar playing. There are many players and a lot of material to learn. The few who become great will be those with the ability to transform themselves from followers to leaders, while retaining and adding depth to their own particular sound. I wrote this book because I want you to take what I've given and become a leader. Let your fingers fly where they may; my knowledge is no more than the result of my curiosity and a strong desire to make my sound say what was in my heart. Let each bit of information become like stones. Use them to build, and remember that none of us learns everything all at once. There is a time and a place for each bit of knowledge, and the right lick at the right time can be absolutely priceless.

I can recall one special day when I was home alone playing like crazy (I never thought of it as practicing). I suddenly looked at the fingerboard and said to myself, "My God, you really *do* know this thing! Not only that, but you can *speak* with it!" I was about seventeen at the time, and what I really was expressing was the reaching of a plateau in my playing, a coming of age. There have since been many more realizations and plateaus, but none so deeply affecting as that first big one, when I truly felt connected to my instrument.

The electric guitar can be a great means of personal expression for you. In this book I chose to share some of what I consider to be the most important bits of information and music that I know, pertaining to the electric guitar.

In an indirect way, I've also shared with you the joys of my learning experience with these arrangements of notes that I discovered on records, on stages, in old rehearsal halls, in bars, in my room as a teenager, and even while teaching someone else.

All this means a lot to me. However, the most rewarding thing of all is sharing knowledge and joy with you. You now have the information you need to further your own guitar playing and to help shape the future of music in the process. Good luck!

Discography

To further aid in your learning process, the study of important recordings involving the electric guitar is essential. The following is a list, broken down into several categories, of what I consider to be some of the most crucial albums for you to hear during your development as an electric guitarist.

BLUES

Michael Bloomfield
(with the Paul Butterfield Blues Band)
The Paul Butterfield Blues Band, Elektra
(with Bob Dylan)
Highway 61 Revisited, Columbia
Blonde on Blonde, Columbia

Buddy Guy
A Man and the Blues, Vanguard

Albert King, Otis Rush
Door to Door, Chess

B.B. King
Completely Well, ABC Bluesway
Lucille, ABC Bluesway

Magic Sam
West Side Soul, Delmark

T-Bone Walker
Stormy Monday Blues, ABC Bluesway

COUNTRY

Roy Nichols
(with Merle Haggard)
Pride in What I Am, Capitol
Let Me Tell You About a Song, Capitol
Mama Tried, Capitol

Carl Perkins
Greatest Hits, Columbia
(with Paul McCartney)
Tug of War, Columbia

Jerry Reed
When You're Hot You're Hot, RCA
Me and Chet, RCA

Merle Travis
The Best of Merle Travis, Capitol
The Merle Travis Guitar, Capitol
Strictly Guitar, Capitol

Clarence White
(with the Byrds)
Younger Than Yesterday, Columbia
Ballad of Easy Rider, Columbia
(Untitled), Columbia

RHYTHM AND BLUES

Chuck Berry
Chuck Berry's Golden Decade, Chess

Steve Cropper
(with Otis Redding)
The Dock of the Bay, ATCO
The Immortal Otis Redding, ATCO
(with Booker T. and the MGs)
Green Onions, Stax-Volt

Bo Diddley
Go Bo Diddley, Checker
Have Guitar, Will Travel, Checker

Cornell Dupree
(with King Curtis and the Kingpins)
King Curtis Live at the Fillmore West, ATCO

ROCK

Jeff Beck
Truth, Epic
Beck-Ola, Epic
There and Back, Epic
Blow by Blow, Epic

Eric Clapton
461 Ocean Boulevard, RSO
Slowhand, RSO
(with John Mayall)
Bluesbreakers, London
(with the Yardbirds)
For Your Love, Epic
Having a Rave Up with the Yardbirds, Epic
(with Cream)
Fresh Cream, ATCO
Disraeli Gears, ATCO
Wheels of Fire, ATCO
(with Derek and the Dominoes)
Layla, ATCO

George Harrison
(with the Beatles)
All Beatles records and solo LPs
(with Eric Clapton)
The Concert for Bangladesh, Apple

Jimi Hendrix
Are You Experienced?, Reprise
Electric Ladyland, Reprise
Axis: Bold as Love, Reprise

John Lennon
All Beatles records and solo LPs

Jimmy Page
All Led Zeppelin albums.

Keith Richards
(with the Rolling Stones)
Out of Our Heads, London
Beggars Banquet, London
Let It Bleed, London
Sticky Fingers, ATCO

Peter Townshend
(with the Who)
Happy Jack, Decca
The Who Sell Out, Decca
Tommy, Decca

SLIDE GUITAR

Duane Allman
(with the Allman Brothers)
Eat a Peach, Capricorn
Beginnings, Capricorn
An Anthology, Capricorn

Elmore James
Whose Muddy Shoes, Chess

Mick Taylor
(with the Rolling Stones)
Let It Bleed, London
Sticky Fingers, ATCO

Rob Stoner, Joan Baez, Bob Dylan, Eric Andersen,
and Arlen Roth. (Mary Alfieri)

Ramblin' Jack Elliott, Eric Andersen, Arlen Roth, circa
1976. (Mary Alfieri)

Albert Lee, Arlen Roth, Phil Kubicki, and James Burton. (Deborah Smith)

Telecaster madness: Steve Morse, Arlen Roth, and Albert Lee. (Deborah Smith)

ABOUT THE AUTHOR

Arlen Roth has spent most of his life playing the guitar. Over the past fifteen years, he has become one of the world's foremost guitarists/educators. He completed the 1983 world tour as Simon and Garfunkel's lead guitarist and started working on his fourth album and the plans for his own world tour of performances and clinics.

To date, Arlen has recorded three highly acclaimed solo LPs: *Guitarist, Hot Pickups,* and *Paint Job.* He has performed on numerous television and movie sound tracks and has appeared on "Saturday Night Live" and in the Bob Dylan film *Reynaldo and Clara.*

Arlen's three previous books on slide guitar, Nashville guitar, and blues guitar are all top sellers, and he is a featured monthly columnist for *Guitar Player* magazine. He has also published articles in *Frets, Musician, Guitar World,* and *Circus* magazines. Arlen's own "Hot Licks" instruction tapes go out to students all over the world.

Arlen lives in New York with his wife, Deborah, and their new baby.

Sound check with Simon and Garfunkel on a hot afternoon in one of America's ballparks. (Deborah Smith)